fun••

Longmans, Green
and Company
Toronto and New York

Making your living is

●●●●●● *fun*

by Kate Aitken

Longmans, Green and Company
20 Cranfield Road, Toronto 16

Longmans, Green & Co. Inc.,
119 West 40th Street, New York 18

Longmans Green & Co. Ltd.,
6-7 Clifford St., London W.I

First Edition 1959

Printed and bound in Canada
By The Hunter Rose Co. Limited

Contents

Introduction

THOMAS HARDY, well-known British novelist, just before he died, walked in the twilight over his native Wessex hills. The evening was dull and the sky sullen. The fading light, the falling leaves, the death of summer sent him home in a characteristic mood of deep despair. That night he wrote these words: "After all, life is so short and most of it taken up in the struggle for bare existence."

Here showed the temperament of a tragic, fatalistic man. I am neither tragic nor fatalistic and certainly no Thomas Hardy. Throughout my life time I've gone blithely into a dozen different ways of earning a living, every one of them an adventure. Some paid off, others left me so broke that I didn't know where to turn for the next penny. But successful or not, they all added up to stimulating, interesting experiences. The recollection of so many human beings, so many enterprises—just recounting them brings back the smell of printer's ink, the glaring lights of a fashion runway, the tender colour of an apple orchard in bloom, chalk dust, and that pervasive odour that goes with small boys whose pockets are filled with broken pencils, fish worms, and dirty hard candy.

And here's an amazing thing about making a living. If we had a rigid formula for success we would all be riding on the crest of a wave and life would be very dull. It's only by trial and error that we find out what pays and what doesn't pay. Too, this condition can vary from season to season, from year to year. But usually financial losses are offset by the thrill of trying something new, something different, learning the hard way. The zest of launching into a new, untried field more than compensates for the agony of birth pangs. Even if the whole project dies on its feet you still have left the experience gained and the ability to cut your losses.

So here's to the gay adventurers ready to try anything once, smart enough to wipe out a mistake, and with never a backward look. To these fortunate people life is always tomorrow with its lure of "Let's try something else."

part one••

PART ONE

Chapter one

Comes the first penny

Do you remember how you earned your first penny, and far more important, how you spent it? I do; it was my first lesson in finance. My father owned a country store in a small village, and since the house was part of the building, we were brought up in the midst of that ordered confusion. There were seven children, and the milliner, the tailor, the dressmaker and the store help all lived with us. Some of the school-teachers boarded at our place, so that under one roof there were twenty-three of us. That life taught us not only to be self-sufficient, but that in emergencies it was team work that counted. Even as children we realized that if our parents gave us healthy bodies and a good education, we were expected to make our own way in the world. One by one we left the shelter of home, embarking on separate careers.

My life has been particularly interesting. I've sold cosmetics and flour, taught school and raised hens, conducted cooking schools and done fashion commentating, written books and gone into radio and TV, all of it thanks to my early training. Being the first girl in a large family of boys, I was taught to cook by my mother. Helping in the store I learned fabrics, textiles, colours. With a father who read aloud to us incessantly I learned the beauty of words. But best of all, in this widely assorted group in which we grew up we learned to talk up or were talked under, but always with politeness. And outside home, with competition from two other general stores, good public relations was part of our background.

Although my mother was a wonderful cook and with plenty of imagination, store cookies at the bake shop always fascinated me. When mother ran out of home-made bread and I was sent

I

to Stewart's for the occasional loaf, I drooled at the sight of those fancy biscuits filled with sweet icing. I spent my first earnings on a whole pound of them.

And how did I earn the money for these delicacies?

On the wooded hills overlooking our village wild raspberries grew in great abundance. Long before I was allowed to go on the berry-picking expeditions, my brothers would sally forth in the dew-laden morning, and come back with loaded pails which father bought for the store at three cents a pound. Then came the great day when I too was allowed to pack a lunch, take along a little tin pail and go berry picking. Before eight o'clock we were soaked to the skin with dew and it was scratchy work. It seemed as if the bottom of the pail would never get covered, but gradually it filled up. We came home at noon and had our berries weighed, and my little container netted me fifteen cents.

Mother always had dinner ready on the table for us; and throughout the whole meal that money burned a hole in my pocket. The minute the dishes were washed (and in our house we all helped) I slid quietly out of the cook-house door, rushed up the street and bought me a whole pound of those marvellous biscuits. What happened? My mother, with eyes in the back of her head, saw me coming in with my contraband goods, stopped me dead in my tracks, fixed me with a stern eye and said, "Katie, what have you got in that bag?"

"Store cookies," I answered, my head hanging.

"Where did you get them?"

"The bake shop."

"Hand them over," said my mother. "In this house we all share. We'll have them for supper."

That's exactly what happened. That night at the supper table my store of cookies was handed around, but when the plate came to me I couldn't even look at them—just murmured "No thank you." But my father, while thoroughly enjoying his store cookies, pounded home my first hard lesson in the field of finance.

"Easy come, easy go, Katie," he said between nibbles. "You'll never get along in the world that way."

To this day store cookies have no appeal for me.

The itinerant milliners in our general store always lived in the house with us, their board and lodging deducted from the wages paid. They came, these gorgeous city-bred creatures, for the spring and fall season. One spring our milliner was a young widow who, as a side line, sold cosmetics, almost unknown in those days. But she did very well. When she left at the end of June she bequeathed the business to me, although I was only twelve years old. I inherited her kit with its samples of face creams, powder, hand lotion, perfume, hair tonic and perfumed soap. Along with the kit went the order forms and price lists of the city firm to whom all orders were remitted. On a purely speculative basis I rented a bicycle and started out selling cosmetics.

What a saleswoman! My face had never known powder, my hands were tanned and still scratched from berry picking, and the selling outfit was a simple cotton dress from which black stockinged legs emerged like pipe stems; but the customers were wonderful. They gave me orders, possibly to get rid of me or possibly because within every woman's heart is the desire to be beautiful. Nowadays, reading in the slick magazines the high-priced copy promoting every beauty aid, I think, "But the patter's just the same. Soft hands, youthful skin, alluring eyes and lustrous hair. Every woman's dream."

Even the minister's wife succumbed to the lure sufficiently to buy a box of powder. The reverend gentleman descended on my father like a ton of bricks, asking in an angry voice, "Do you know, Robert, how that child of yours sold my wife that powder? She quoted the Song of Solomon. She's too young to read that."

During that hot summer, all July and August, I cycled up and down sandy country roads, braved farm-house dogs and toured the village. The orders went in, the goods were delivered and the money, or its equivalent in butter and eggs, collected. The trade and barter items I sold to Father, but I trusted no one with the money. It was kept under my bed in a tin box. And when school opened the first week in September I was the proud possessor of $27.85. That was the year I went into High School, and I was able to pay for my own books. Then came the great news! The old cosmetic kit, battered, beaten up, was

3

mine for keeps. The sample face cream was rancid, the powder box half empty and the perfume bottle pretty well exhausted. But the whole array was set up on my bureau. Every time I looked at those magic aids to beauty I felt like a woman of the world.

Chapter two

A new world opens

HIGH school, so divorced from public school, was as thrilling as the first-night opening of a new play. Although all grades were housed in the same building, the high-school students felt themselves a race apart. We had passed our entrance exams. We had new books and had entered into a world of Latin and physics, algebra and Euclid, and quite impressive homework. It was in high school I got my first taste of being a teacher.

In our small village there were no supply teachers. So when Miss Mitchell, who taught the second room in public school, was laid low with a cold I was nominated as the fill-in. Miss Mitchell, tall and dignified, wore a dress that came right to the floor. This fourteen-year-old substitute teacher, with her hair down her back, was so well known to all the youngsters as Katie Scott that they thought this was a game and tried all their tricks. But since I had tried them on the teacher myself I knew what they were up to. For three happy days it was give and take on the noisy battle-ground of the second room. But the last day, Friday, was when I made the headlines.

Friday afternoon in any schoolroom is a period of unrest. It's hard to make youngsters settle down. We did exercises, we sang; then finally, at my wit's end, I said, "Let's go out under the trees and tell stories." Some of the children thus released dashed down to the village to spread the glad news. Parents and school trustees came up to the school and looked over the fence to see what was going on. The consensus was that school-teaching had gone to the dogs.

But out of that adventure I got a new understanding of children and of the way a taxpayer looks at his money, and $6.oo in cash. The money bought the material for a new dress, which I still remember—soft, brown, silky material with white stripes. Mother made it up for me to wear to my music examination. No dress ever since worn has given me the same sense of pride that little brown frock provided. I had paid for it myself.

An old stone school where teachers were trained, the little red school-house set in the midst of farm lands, the yellow brick village school, the weather-beaten clapboard prairie school, the big impersonal city school—all these I knew during seven happy years of teaching. It was a life so rich and rewarding that even now when September rolls around, a wave of homesickness sweeps over me, a nostalgia for children and the smell of chalk.

Nowadays when every parent plans for the youngsters a university education, it seems incredible that with only sixteen years of life to my credit and exactly three months of training, I launched into this interesting career.

Our nearest teacher-training school was in Bradford, a sizeable town, twelve miles from our village. There was no railway connection, so the journey that fall was made Monday morning and Friday night by bicycle. The hills were steep and the way was rough, but every road was bordered with maples, red from the autumn frosts, and every fence corner was aglow with wild aster and goldenrod.

We studied theory in the morning, taught practice lessons in the afternoon. All the school children knew we didn't amount to much as teachers, and tried all the foxy tricks in their quite adequate repertoire to make fools of us in front of the senior, qualified teachers. But before Christmas holidays we graduated.

Three months' training! Now to find a school board brave enough to take on an inexperienced teacher such as myself. The day after Christmas I landed a job—a small country school, fourteen miles from a railroad and with a reputation of having the toughest aggregation of boys in the whole township. There were eight grades, thirty-eight pupils, a blackboard, chalk, two brushes and a teacher's desk. The pupil's desks were battle-scarred and ink-stained. The wood-burning stove was at the back of the

6

room, and when the stove-pipes got red hot, they leaked great gobs of varnish that dropped on the unwary like old-fashioned H-bombs. The big boys were taller than I and much tougher. Every time I walked up and down the aisles I felt as if I were walking on a tight-rope. So out of my huge salary of $325 a year—$32.50 a month—I spent $3.00 on a strap. (The previous teacher had carefully removed his).

If you've never lived in a small, rather isolated community, you might imagine it takes news a long time to travel. Not in this community. The local post office, which was also the general store and a country club, was the unofficial broadcast station. All day Saturday the teacher's strap was a topic of conversation. "That little bit of a thing! She wouldn't dast use it." All of which was relayed back to me.

Monday morning was the testing time. The biggest boy in the school lipped me. And with every ounce of strength that my young body possessed, I whaled him. That was the last time I used the strap. I never needed it again.

Although brought up in a small village, I had never known farm life intimately; now I was part of it. Milking time and the smell of clover hay; the hiss of the milk as it foamed in the pail; the little streams that became raging torrents as the snow melted; the first soft green of the fields; the clack of the mower as the green hay fell in soft swathes. Years later I read a phrase which completely summed up that winter and spring—"The fresh, fair winds of freedom."

A friendly community this, which nightly gathered in the corner store, planned sleigh rides, dances, euchre parties and church suppers in which everyone was included. The funerals were as much community get-togethers as the parties. Indeed when it was an important funeral, the school was closed for the afternoon. There were none of today's rather dreadful trappings of death, and no farmer's wife came to the house of mourning without a boiled ham, a batch of cookies or a cake, all of which were thoroughly enjoyed. Funerals were like old boys' reunions.

The family with whom I lived always boarded the teacher, who slept on a feather tick in a little bedroom off the parlour. All winter the parlour stove was kept burning and it was teacher's

7

prerogative to dress, undress, and bathe in hot soft water right by the stove. I put a huge pan of water on the stove last thing at night, hopped out shivering in the morning, poked up the fire, then gradually and happily thawed out.

Throughout the winter, since we were far from cities, our food was plain and simple—oatmeal porridge with brown sugar, meat, potatoes, root vegetables, preserves, pickles, pie and cake. But our Mrs. McCubbin kept hens who loafed all winter, then began to lay when March madness hit them. The first fresh eggs, home-made bread, wild strawberry jam—they were our Festival of Spring.

Mr. McCubbin was the local blacksmith and Saturdays all the farmers brought their horses in to be shod. The rosy glow of the open fire, the bright red horseshoes hammered into place, the incessant and friendly gossip were all part of this new experience. Did the farmers like having me around the blacksmith shop? I'll say they didn't, but gradually they got accustomed to me. Their talk of crops and cattle, of weather and prices, of roads and fences was like a soap opera since it was always full of drama. Would Bill's cow get better? Was the winter wheat killed out? Shouldn't John Smith do something about that wild kid of his, chasing all over the countryside with a different girl in the cutter every night? How much money did the Ladies Aid make at their pancake supper? Tranquil? Never. Just one episode after another, each as important as a presidential election.

After six months' teaching I went home with $96.00 in my pocket and a feeling of belonging.

That summer the teacher of the junior room in our hometown school decided to quit. The race was on. Teachers weren't scarce but jobs were. So it all boiled down to who would take the smallest salary. The chairman of the school board figured that if I were living at home, with no board to pay, I should come pretty cheap. So early one morning he drove up to the house, called me over to the buggy and said, "Katie, how would you like to teach the junior room?" Flattered and flustered, I said, "Oh, Mr. Strangeways, I'd love it!"

"What did you get at the last school?"

8

"$325 a year."

"Well," he said meditatively, "I think we can do a little better than that. We're quite prepared, because of your father and mother, to give you $375 a year."

$50 raise! I jumped at it. At that time there was no Teachers' Federation, there was no contract. On the first day of September I simply started to teach. It wasn't until months afterwards that I learned the next bid was $450.

Throwing away the taxpayers' money—here is one of the catch phrases of today, whether applied to the Pentagon, the city hall or a new bridge. This was the criticism directed against me in the new job. The four-room school was old. The junior room, in which I taught, was downstairs, had windows set so high that even the teacher couldn't see out. There was no play equipment for the 50 children in that one room, all under eight years old.

I went to the school-board meeting with quite a modest request—twenty pounds of coloured clay, ten yards of curtaining, coloured sticks and squares, and a drop-leaf table at which the children could work. "Unheard of," said the trustees, "it's throwing money away!"

Finally the order did go through. Did it pay? There was a retarded youngster in the room, six years old. In the yard the children teased him, poked fun at him. One day in a fit of rage and frustration he pulled a little jack-knife out of his pocket and began stabbing madly. Indignant parents said. "Take him out of school, he's a menace." But the school board insisted that he be given a chance. That same week the coloured clay came, the new water colours, the sticks, the blocks. The local carpenter put up the hinged table, and there the little fellow would sit, modelling cats and dogs, hens and pigs to his heart's content and very cleverly. The much debated supplies were a human success.

After two years in the junior room I decided if I were ever going to make real money—$500 a year—an extra teaching certificate was needed. So I took a more advanced teacher-training course and graduated at Easter.

9

All winter I'd been reading romantic stories of the West and discovered that back from the main line of rail and in the ranching districts, so-called summer teachers were needed. Those were the days before motor cars and paved highways were part of our way of life. Trails meandered across the prairie turning off to the big ranches. When the crop of youngsters was sufficiently great a school-house was centred in each district. But because the ranches were so far from town, because all the children rode horseback to school, because winter storms were so tempestuous and snow so deep, schools opened in April, closed with the first big blow. Here, I thought, was my chance to see, to meet, to talk to these dashing cowboys and ranching heroes. Application after application was sent out; eventually I hit the jackpot at Cypress Hills, where five ranchers bred and raised horses.

I left our small village with great expectations and headed for the wide open spaces. The train journey took four days and four nights on a tourist train packed with men, women and children. We slept in wooden bunks and cooked our own meals on a coal-burning stove at one end of the car. My mother had packed enough food for a journey round the world, and when mealtime came it was the grand switch.

"Like a piece of my pie?"

"I sure would. Here, have one of my cookies." The children were getting handouts all the time. This was pretty heady excitement for an eighteen-year-old girl who had never been on a sleeper before and who thought the wooden bunk was almost like a private suite. To top it off, the train ran into a rock slide. We had to be shunted off on a siding, where we spent the night waiting for the next avalanche. This added bit of excitement delayed the train eight hours.

But on a Sunday morning, the first day of April, we arrived at Maple Creek, my take-off point for the Cypress Hills. I was dumped off the train, bag and baggage, and not a soul was in sight except the station agent. He paid no attention to me until the train had dwindled far down the track. Then he tossed my trunk on the truck, wheeled it up to me and said, "You the new school-teacher, Cypress Hills?"

"Yes," I answered, "and Mr. Pollock was to meet me."

"Here yesterday," said the agent laconically, talking like a teletype machine. "Told him the train was late . . . said he couldn't stay . . . told me to get you a buckboard . . . it's a fourteen-mile drive . . . better wait in the station."

Have you ever sat in a deserted waiting-room, absolutely alone and feeling as friendless as a lost hound dog? It was only pride that kept me from breaking down and bawling. But the buckboard came, propelled (and that's the right word) by a team of wild ranch horses. The youngster who drove it took one look at my Merry Widow hat, then said, "Better take it off miss, wind's kind of high."

Agent and driver loaded in my trunk. I climbed over the front wheels into the seat and away we went down the main street of the little town, past the shacks at the outskirts, then off across the prairie trail. The minute we hit the open country the gophers began popping out of their holes, and one gopher was enough to set this team haring down the home stretch. The boy drove; I hung on. Then came a particularly mad dash. The buckboard rocked and rolled, the back flew down, my trunk fell off and burst open; and flying across the prairie like tumbleweed went bloomers, petticoats, shoes, stockings, school books, everything I owned. It took us an hour to round up the contents of the trunk. A most embarrassing hour! The young driver, a modest soul, thought he shouldn't pick up a lady's underwear so he would look the other way while I bundled together the unmentionables.

The sun was setting when we finally arrived at the ranch house which was to be my home. For hours we'd been buckboarding across prairies, desolate as last summer's hat, manoeuvring through gullies and seeing not one human habitation. Then suddenly the wide-spreading ranch house, the door flung open, and the greeting with which I was to become so familiar, "Light, stranger, come in and eat." That was my introduction to Cypress Hills, an ex-Mountie settlement.

Red-coated Mounties, members of the Royal Canadian Mounted Police, are known the world over. You see them in movies, acting as escort to royalty, guarding the Canadian Embassy at Washington. This is only show-window duty. But this famous force was organized to administer justice, to preserve law and order in the newly opened West. A military organization with the wild tang of adventure, it attracted young men from all parts of the British Empire. Barracks were set up at strategic points. Mounties were taught to ride, to shoot, to chart a course, to camp, to trek into every part of the great Northwest. After seven years' duty, the recruit could then leave the force or join up permanently.

The five ranchers in the Cypress Hills district were all ex-Mounties. An Irishman, a Scotsman, an American, an Englishman and a Canadian. They all loved horses, all bought huge grants of land at fifty cents an acre to raise them. All married and established families, and it was their children whom I had been hired to teach starting Monday morning.

Nothing in my correspondence with Trustee Pollock had indicated that the school-house was three miles from the ranch house at which I lived, that every one of the thirteen pupils, scattered over an area of fifteen miles, rode to school, and that teacher was also expected to ride horseback. After breakfast that first day, when three saddled horses were led up to the kitchen door, when Margaret and Gordon, the youngsters in the house, swung up on their horses and expected me to follow suit, I didn't know on which side to mount. It was scramble, scramble into the saddle like a tenderfoot, then hang on for dear life. How I ever achieved that three-mile ride I'll never know.

When we arrived at the five-strand barbed-wire fence that enclosed the school-yard, the children lifted their horses clear over with never a hoof click. But I slid off my horse and shamelessly crawled under the fence. And from this undignified position I got my first look at the weather-beaten frame school, its foundation piled with sod and weighted down with stones. It didn't take long to discover the reason for that precaution. The Cypress Hills climbed steeply upward to the flat plateau on top of the range. To the south lay the heights of Montana, between lay a vast canyon (a paradise for cattle rustlers) down which the wind swooped fiercely for weeks on end. Along the narrow trail on top of what the youngsters called the Hog's Back the wind always blew. Sometimes, going home after school, the blast was so strong we would have to dismount and walk along sheltered by the horses.

Inside, the school was not much more prepossessing than outside. It had been shut up for five months, and hastily cleaned by the youngsters; and there they were waiting for me, their horses all hitched to the fence. A strange teacher, strange pupils. They eye one another warily. Is she going to be cranky? You can see the question in their eyes. Are they going to be hard to handle?—that was the question in my mind. But what eased the situation for all of us was that they taught me how to ride. Here was I, a greenhorn, and here were they, experts, since most of them rode horseback as soon as they could walk. That first recess when we all walked out into the school-yard, the Pollock children took a look at my horse and the saddle. "Is that your saddle, teacher?"

"No," said Gordon, "that's Willie's saddle. Teacher ain't got a saddle.

"Did Willie lend his saddle to teacher?"

And with that brief interchange I learned that every Western teacher should come equipped not only with text-books but also with a saddle. Horses were plentiful—anyone would lend you a horse; but a saddle is as individual and as personal as grandpa's false teeth. So a saddle I had to get. Mr. Pollock, who was going to town that week, offered to buy me one. "How much?" I asked.

"Well," answered my trustee, "I could get you a nice little saddle for $60."

He might just as well said a million dollars, since I had exactly $10 in my purse. But he bought me a saddle, took it off my pay of $50 a month. Mrs. White, another rancher's wife, made me a divided riding skirt, floor length, the accepted Western riding costume. Even on that first ride to school I had discovered that a tight suit skirt wasn't just the thing for horseback riding.

Now all I had to do was learn to ride. As the lessons continued, better horses were forthcoming. The first one, an old white nag, was almost as broad as long, but was steady. Within two or three weeks I had graduated to a narrower type; by the end of two months I could sail over the barbed-wire fence on a

13

real pinto pony along with the youngsters. But quite frankly, for the first month I slept more comfortably face down.

That was one of the happiest six months of my life. We rode the range, we went to neighbourhood dances, we shot coyotes, the prairie version of riding to hounds. The teaching was not strenuous, broken up as it was with what might be called extra-mural activities, including the semi-annual shopping spree at Maple Creek, a day's expedition. All these I remember; and above all I remember my love for this vast open country. We had the encircling vastness of the prairies, broken only by trails. Behind us were the purple hills, clothed in tall jack pine, and above was the plateau, dotted with innumerable lakes. Nowadays when I fly over this prairie country in the springtime I see the prairie grass, dry as tinder with not a blade of green. But I know that with May will come the quick greening, the overnight blooming of the wild roses.

In this ranch country, through which no rivers or streams ran and where the rainfall was light, wheat farming was unknown. The ranch wife tried to make a small garden, but the water for that had to be brought down from the hills in open wooden flumes. There were no lawns to mow, no flower beds to weed; and since the horses were on range until the fall roundup, life in the spring was leisurely.

So it was in May that the semi-annual shopping took place for both the Pollock and the White families. Mr. and Mrs. Pollock, Mrs. White and the youngest children travelled in the wagon, the rest of us went on horseback. Tall, rangy ex-Mountie Pollock, still sporting the army-type handle-bar moustache, handled the reins of his thoroughbred percherons. On the other side perched gentle little Mrs. Pollock, about the size of a sparrow; and between them, acting as a cushion, was Scottish-born Mrs. White, white-haired, rosy-cheeked and comfortable. The children sprawled on the hay in the back of the wagon.

This day-long adventure started shortly after sunrise and ended at sunset. The two women shopped in the one general store, and settled down comfortably with yard-long lists through which they worked their way; the next shopping day was six months off. Bags of flour, sacks of sugar, cases of vegetables, dried fruits, canned fruits, overalls, yard goods, coal oil, yeast, tinware, soap—just everything a big family would use. It was not unusual for each family to spend well over a thousand dollars on that one shopping expedition. And the system of finance would make a modern merchant tear his hair; these huge amounts were carried on the books until after the fall roundup when the young horses were sold.

At last it was over; every item was checked off the list. The wagon was piled high. Then came the treat of the afternoon. There were no movies, no parks, no entertainment, but there was an ice-cream parlour with small wooden tables, wire-back chairs and a hitching bar in front. It was "Dish her out Sam, as much as they can eat." Home-made ice cream, creamy yellow and rich as butter, was piled high in saucers and consumed to the last melting spoonful, with the baby eating as much as a grown-up.

And then we were off. When the loaded wagon lumbered down the dusty streets in the late afternoon the children were packed in wherever they would fit. Around the wagon was an entourage of outriders, the girls in riding skirts and the cowboys in their ten-gallon hats and white chaps. On the street every head turned, which was a signal for each rider to rein in his horse until each well-trained mount was standing on his hind feet. Cecil B. DeMille could have made a movie of it.

But the shopping didn't end with this semi-annual spree. Every ranch house received mail-order catalogues from Dublin, from Edinburgh and from London. Since it took six months from the time the order was mailed overseas until the goods arrived, Christmas shopping was done in July; summer shopping round about Christmas. The jams, the tartans, the tweeds, the expensive tea all came from overseas. Nowadays luxuries and specialty goods are flown back and forth across the ocean so casually that we take them for granted. But at that time, when the huge wooden crates finally arrived at the small rail depot of Maple Creek, Saskatchewan, it was a miracle of transport. Carefully packed overseas, the goods had to withstand the pitching and tossing in the ship's hold, and the freight journey of three thousand miles. It was another odyssey.

Since our mail at Cypress Hills was delivered only once a week, the news usually came with a neighbour.

"Hey Dave," he would say to Mr. White, "that shipment's here from overseas. Four crates." So in again would go the ranch wagon. The crates were loaded at the station and brought out to the ranch house. When the crowbar and the nail-puller had done their work, when the packages were lifted out, it was just as if Selfridge's, Saks Fifth Avenue, Neiman-Marcus and Henry Morgan's had come to Cypress Hills.

Grown-ups, children and ranch hands all gathered round the big kitchen table, and not a lick of work was done until the last parcel was opened. Coping with the pushing and shoving of the excited children, Mr. White reverted to his original barracks-room training. When the language became too colourful, Mrs. White would interject gently, "Now, now Mr. White, remember the children."

And not the least of the excitement was the reading of the six-months-old copies of the Edinburgh *Scotsman*, the *Yorkshire Post* or the Dublin *Irish Times* used in packing the parcels. Every newspaper was carefully laid out on the table and read inch by inch. Mr. Pollock, who thought nothing of paying $2,000 for a brood mare, always turned to the livestock sales. But the women turned to the Births, Deaths and Marriages and would argue interminably as to whether or not the late deceased was related to their branch of the MacIntosh family.

The foodstuffs were stored in the pantry, the yard goods carefully put away in the bedrooms and the gifts distributed immediately. It was less trouble than wrapping them.

As soon as the snow was off the ground the dance season was in full swing, with every ranch taking its turn. Many of the ranch wives hadn't seen one another all winter and were keen as mustard for a visit. No special invitations were issued. The men, riding from one ranch to the other, would say casually, "The Hamiltons are having a dance Thursday night." That was enough; the whole family went along. Again Dad and Mother rode in the wagon, with the toddlers bedded down in the back. Under the wagon seat, and well protected, were the salmon sandwiches, the cookies, the tarts and the cakes, a supply so generous that there was not only enough for the family but also for the visiting bachelors. On arrival at the ranch house the women carefully carried the food to the kitchen, casually unwrapped it, then stood back waiting for the inevitable comment, "Oh Mrs. Fritz, you do make the most wonderful chocolate cake," or "Butter tarts! I'll bet they'll melt in your mouth." By nine o'clock the kitchen looked like one of the restaurants whose slogan was "All you can eat for $1.00," except that the price tag was missing.

In the meantime the men took the horses to the corral, unsaddled them, then proceeded to slick up. Chaps were hung on the stable pegs, hair was plastered down with water, bow ties adjusted and riding boots wiped clean of dust.

In the spare bedroom the girls slipped out of their riding skirts, got into light dresses, (a little rumpled from being carried in saddle bags), dusted on a bit of cornstarch over shiny noses and were ready to go. After all this titivating the room was left free for the babies. They were parked on the big double bed and left to howl themselves to sleep.

The children dashed from corral to house trying to look as grown-up as possible so that they too might be included in the dancing. The shrill sawing of bow on strings as the fiddlers tuned up did nothing to lessen the din.

Every dance started the same way, with a Paul Jones in which everyone joined. Then came the complicated square dances, which took years to learn. The caller-off sat on a chair on top of the kitchen table and put us through six involved sets. What with the stamping, the shouting and the general hullaballoo, it took a strong floor to stand up against the onslaught.

It was just about now that the older men quietly faded away. This was the moment for which they had been waiting; the keg of beer in the barn was broached. But in this rather casual life there were still certain rigid conventions—never any beer for the women, and never a drink for the younger males until after midnight, when discipline was somewhat relaxed. Another amusing unwritten law was this: with no indoor plumbing, the outdoor facilities, complete with neat squares of newspaper, were reserved for the fair sex.

Sharp at twelve the feast was served. Piled on the long table was the food that everyone had provided; boiling on the stove were gallons of coffee. We ate, we drank coffee until everyone was happy and satisfied. When the last mouthful had been swallowed the male contingent took off to the barn and the weaker sex washed up the dishes.

Since riding at night in gopher-infested country was hazardous, we danced until the sun came up. It was so easy in the darkness for the horse to put his foot in a gopher hole, throw his rider and break his own leg. But with the dawn we started for home.

The sleeping children were lifted into the wagons, the horses were saddled, and away we went—but not before some rancher's wife had said, "Come over to our place next week."

The Cypress Hills crowd took off together from the Hamilton dance. We were a few miles along the trail when Mrs. Pollock looked over her shoulder to count the children in the back of the wagon. Consternation! Johnny was missing. So back we went to the Hamiltons', searched for Johnny, and found him fast asleep under the spare bed. He'd rolled or been pushed off sometime during the night.

After that first dance I got home with only enough time to take a bath, tidy up and whip down to the school-house. Not a youngster turned up. I sat behind the desk dozing until ten o'clock, then one of the ranchers, who happened to be passing by, came in. "Shucks," he said, "someone should have told you. The day after a dance the school's never open." And it seemed logical, since every pupil had been at the dance and was probably sound asleep.

In our school section were only five families, with thirteen children of school age, none of whom took education too seriously. After all, they were in school only seven months of the year. But since the school was used as a Sunday school from the first Sunday in May, it had to be properly cleaned. At this job the youngsters worked like beavers. There was no use doing anything with the outside; it was too weather-beaten. But we decided, with the consent of the school board, to give the inside a coat of pale grey paint, and one of the ranchers rode into town for paint and brushes. Followed three days of scrubbing, painting, polishing windows, scouring desks, blacking the stove, varnishing the stove-pipes, getting everything ready for the Sunday-school opening. Finally (and this was the last touch of elegance), one of the parents made window boxes, in which we planted geranium slips. Never were house plants so pampered. Happily and cheerfully the youngsters lugged water from the well to water them. And when the first bloom appeared an orchid wouldn't have received the same worshipful attention. But the scented geraniums came to a sad end.

Remote as we were and so few in number, we had no regular minister, but Sunday school was held in the school at three o'clock in the afternoon. A very informal session was this, with one of the ranchers reading a chapter of scripture and everyone repeating the Lord's Prayer. Then followed a few familiar hymns, with Teacher playing the asthmatic old organ with the C sharp silent. The young people came on horseback, and presumably the horses were tethered. But one Sunday a half-broken pony got loose, strolled over to the open window, stuck his head in, and nipped off the geraniums. Words were said that day not included in the prayer book.

The actual school work? Fresh from teacher-training school, I was filled with enthusiasm concerning art work, home economics, sewing and properly laid-out lessons. There was no materials on which to build a formal education, so we did our arithmetic lessons in terms of square miles of range country, herds of horses. Our nature study? The depletion of prairie grass and combating insects. History? To these youngsters the rest of Canada was non-existent, let alone the rest of the world. I taught them very little. Indeed it was they who taught me.

Very occasionally the school was visited by an inspector, who came in a buggy, unheralded and unannounced, and settled in for the day. The youngsters, threatened at home with "when the inspector comes", held him in awe. So when, at recess time one June morning, this official was sighted, the youngsters mounted their horses and cantered to the coulee. When the bell rang they rode back, a very subdued lot. Then came the examination of their knowledge. What little they did know faded out of their heads and they stood there dumb. But here was an understanding man, this western inspector. He closed the book, turned to them and said, "All right, let's see how you can ride," and forthwith organized a rodeo. The horsemanship was as excellent as anything seen at the Calgary Stampede.

In July came one of the big events of the summer. My eldest brother Bruce, in the West on business, made a special trip out to see me. One evening he arrived at the ranch house just as we were staging a small riding competition. Instead of the conventional sister Bruce had always known, here was a harum-scarum girl, practising jumping over a barbed-wire fence, and entranced with the West. Being a real city type, his first thought was, "She might fall in love with one of these romantic characters and stay here." That night he talked to me very sternly. "You know, Kate," he said, "you've forgotten how to use your mind. You used to be a smart girl." So in his usually efficient manner brother Bruce took care of that. Directly he returned to what he called civilization he sent me a complete set of Shakespeare, with the admonition "Read it!"

Our mail came only once a week and was delivered to the Fritz ranch, which served as a post office. When this heavy parcel arrived the Fritz children, pupils in the school, gathered round to see me open it. Out tumbled six volumes of William Shakespeare; they were quite certain, as indeed were all the ranchers, that my brother was slightly pixilated.

This intellectual shot in the arm, plus my brother's nagging, made me turn over a new leaf. Lessons were rigidly taught and examination papers were set. To give everyone a square deal the youngsters were allowed to take the examination papers home, brood over them and write the exam the next day. The grown-ups at home soon put an end to that nonsense. "Look," said one of the trustees, "let up on the kids. We worked all night on those darned exam papers." That effort died stillborn and we went back to our slap-happy ways. A little knowledge, we discovered, was not "a dangerous thing" but mighty pleasant. Then too we'd now got into haying, which took every pair of hands.

Although the range horses were never confined and grubbed for themselves, each ranch had its own stable of riding horses (one for each member of the family and a few spares for visitors), which had to be fed. As well there were two or three dairy cows for milk and butter. Ideal feed for the stock was the slough grass and wild hay covering the flat plateau topping the hills. When haying time came school closed. The big boys went ahead with the mowing machine, the ranch women followed up with the chuck wagons, the rest of us went on horseback. All day it was the clack-clack of the mowing machine, the pungent fragrance of the wild hay, the enormous meals and the camping out. But it was round the camp-fire at night that the early experiences of these ex-Mounties were recounted. The pipes were lit, the children would go quiet and the yarning would begin. "Do you remember . . . .?" And here are some of the stories.

The bachelor O.C. of the Maple Creek barracks was a retired colonel from the British Army; his spinster sister kept house for him. County English, she was equally at home in the saddle or in her brother's drawing-room. A canter each day, winter and summer, sun or rain, was part of her daily ritual. According to custom her attendant, one of the young recruits, rode four paces to the rear. Of a day, so the story ran, her horse stumbled and fell, throwing his rider. Shaken loose, her upper plate bit the dust—but where? Without a word the sister remounted, wheeled for home. There she confided her predicament to her brother and retired to her room. Our ranchers, all five of them, were amongst the search party sent out. Needless to say the store teeth were recovered within a short time but not reported; it was too good a holiday to miss. The search party took the rest of the afternoon off, came back just in time for supper with the pearly treasure carefully wrapped in a handkerchief. It was handed to the batman who relayed it to the Colonel, who in turn gave it to his sister through a crack in the door. The next morning the ride went forward as usual. No mention of this mishap was made in the dignified upper circles, but in the barracks room it was counted a highlight, to be told and retold and probably added to with every telling. I got the full treatment.

Then of course there were the tales of cattle rustling in the Cypress Hills area. The deep canyon, which began in the prairies and ran to the height of land, separated Saskatchewan from Montana. Its deep gullies, its wooded hills, made an ideal hideout not only for the cattle rustlers but for the stolen cattle and horses they had driven off the range. In the early days of the Force, one of the most important duties was to hunt down these cattle rustlers and bring them to trial. It was on such a mission that our Mounties were detailed late in March. The first day out the snow was deep and firm; that night they made camp in a secluded coulee with the snow creaking underfoot and the northern lights shooting across the sky. But towards midnight came the soft Chinook wind, melting the snow and making trails impassable for the horses. The Colonel, never one to waste a day even if the men were immobilized, said, "This is the day to wash your underwear." After great buckets of snow were melted the men stripped off the underwear, then scrubbed it with soap and brushes. Lines were strung from tree to tree and the union suits hung up. That night the wind changed again and a chilly blast blew down from the North Pole. When the bugle sounded in the morning the men rose to find each garment frozen solid. It was another lost day while underwear thawed, was dried in front of the fire and donned again. Was the mission successful? As I heard it, a dirtier bunch of rascals was never brought to justice by a cleaner troop of Mounties.

According to the fireside yarns, the penalty for cattle rustling was swift and sudden if the Mounties were not there to take the prisoners into custody for a proper trial.

As the fire burned down and youthful eyes got bigger and bigger, all the horrible details of stringing the culprit up to the nearest tree were recounted. When finally we pulled the blankets up over our heads, even the wind rustling through the grass sent delightful shivers of horror up and down every spine.

As well as stories of past adventures, we had our own rather spectacular contact with the young Mounties from the Maple Creek barracks. Instead of the dashing red coats they now wore khaki on routine duty, but they were still superbly mounted, outstanding horsemen and firm believers in law and order. The legal season for shooting prairie chickens didn't open until October, but in late August and September the young birds were plump, tender and delicious. One Saturday morning we rode up to the plateau, shot a couple of birds and roasted them, to me a new art. The head and feet were taken off, the entrails removed but the feathers left on. Then this plump little three-pounder was thickly coated with wet clay and slowly baked in hot coals. It was the job of the cook to keep raking the coals over the birds until they were tender through and through. Then we pulled them out, stripped off the clay (the feathers came too) and broke the succulent pieces apart in the fingers. There we sat with the hot luscious joints in hand when riding up the hill came a couple of Mounties. Never did birds disappear so fast down a gopher hole, complete with all the evidence of the crime. The men stopped, joined us in a cup of cold tea and stale sandwiches, fully aware of the feast they had ruined. They stayed long enough to make sure that the prairie chickens couldn't be retrieved.

But the Mounties came to our rescue the morning after the big snowstorm. Early in May, out of a grey windswept sky, the snow began to swirl. The older boys in the school, sensing the blizzard, said: "Looks as though we should go home—and fast." By the time we had the horses saddled and our lunch pails picked up, the snow was a driving, blinding mass, almost impenetrable. We decided to all stick together, go up over the Hog's Back and let the horses lead us. When we reached the height the fury of the wind forced us to dismount and walk, hanging on to the stirrups. Then even the horses got lost. Finally we came to a barbed-wire fence, and blindly followed it along until we came into a little opening where stood an abandoned sod cabin. We tied the horses and made our way inside. The straw in the bunks was musty. There was no wood and no food, but there was shelter; here we spent the night. The older children were quite resigned, but the two little five-year-olds whimpered a bit until they were shamed into silence by their elders. We sang, we recited poetry, we told stories and eventually the long night was over. But even by daylight the snow had obliterated every trail and we didn't know where we were. Then, joy of joys, up rode two Mounties. No school that day. At home we were greeted as heroes, almost as if we had been the sole survivors of a great disaster.

During the late summer and early fall everything happened; it was the western equivalent of Harvest Festival. The Saskatoon berries ripened and instead of dried-apple pie we had luscious, juicy Saskatoon pie. The wild ducks in the lakes on the plateau were ready for the shoot and the fall roundup was on.

For the duck shooting we rode up the hills at twilight. The boys slept outside wrapped in blankets, heads on their saddles; the girls in an old soddie—a sod cabin put up years before. We got up at the crack of dawn, crept down to the edge of the lake, and lay there in the wet grass waiting for the ducks to rise in flight. I was the only amateur shot in the party, and one of the young pupils—a tender, sympathetic type—offered to look after me. He gave me a loaded gun, showed me how to sight it, and magnanimously said to the others: "Let Teacher have the first shot." Everyone agreed, knowing full well what that little rascal was up to. The duck rose; Bill said "Now!" I pulled the trigger. It was as if the end of the world had come. That gun had a kick like a bucking bronco.

The roundup? After the mares were bred in the spring they were turned loose and roamed the range. When the young colts were born they trailed after their mothers through a lazy, loafing summer. But then came the reckoning with their owners—the branding. To an easterner it seemed impossible that a few riders could round up that herd of 3,000 horses scattered over this vast grazing country. But most of the ranch hands had been raised to do this type of work, could cut in and out until the herd was headed in one steady stream homeward. In a cloud of dust and with the thunder of hooves the colts were penned in the huge corral. One after one with the whisk of a rope the colts were lassoed, thrown and branded on the hip. Everyone had told me of the romance of the roundup, so along with the small fry I perched on the topmost rail to view the spectacle. But at the first frenzied squeal of the first colt I ran for the house. Necessary? That I knew; for selling purposes the brand was like the hallmark on silver. But fun to watch? Not for me.

Nothing, not even years of absence, can wipe out the remembrance of kindness and hospitality—the cups of tea, the wedges of fresh cake, the "Hi Teacher, come in and light." Perhaps most vivid is this daily scene in the White's big kitchen. Every afternoon Scottish-born Mrs. White made a huge pot of tea and fresh scones. No matter where her husband Dave or the boys were, intuitively they knew when tea was ready. Mrs. White sat at one end of the oilcloth table with the brown teapot beside her, the cups and saucers ranged about. Mr. White sat at the other end and the rest of us scattered about the table, as close to the scones as was humanly possible. But, well trained, we never reached for them until Mr. White got his first cup of tea.

As in the famous Elsie Dinsmore family, Mrs. White in public always addressed her husband as Mr. White. So, with teapot in hand, it would be, "How would you like your tea, Mr. White?"

"Just as it comes from the spout, madam, just as it comes from the spout."

After that the scones were passed.

That fall came news of my father's serious illness. "Come home at once," wired my mother. So I re-packed the trunk, dusted off the Merry Widow sailor, went back by buckboard to the little station, and left Cypress Hills. But does anyone ever leave a place that is well loved? Even today, when we get out the book of old snapshots I can see the limitless prairies and the high green hills, feel the rush of wind as we galloped down the trail, remember by name every youngster in that little school-house.

The financial return from that six months' teaching? Not too good. Mr. Pollock bought back the $60 saddle at half price. I had paid out $90 in board money and bought the material for the riding skirt and blouse. But I did have enough money for my ticket home, this time first class. As my father said to me, "Easy come, easy go."

Young and all as I was on that four-day journey back home, I sensed something of the changes sweeping over the West. The Cypress Hills in which we went duck shooting is now a national park. The trails over which we galloped are now paved roads, straight as a die. The shabby little school-house has been replaced with a handsome structure and the youngsters come to school in a yellow bus instead of on horseback. Ranch houses have their own electric plants; stoves and refrigerators and deep-freeze units are considered necessary equipment. The twelve-mile drive into town is an almost nightly occurrence and shopping is done in a supermarket. Instead of ranch hands riding the range, almost every rancher has his own small plane for scouting purposes. It is a new West; but happily for me I lived in and loved the old.

Chapter three

Home again

MY FATHER died the night I got home. This was the first time death had closely touched our family, but somehow there was nothing terrifying about it. Our parents had always been devoted to one another, indeed had never fallen out of love. Shortly after midnight, Father fell quietly asleep, holding close to Mother's hand, and sighing softly "Anne, Anne."

For two days it was a house of mourning; then of necessity we took stock. Although Father died suddenly, he had not been his usual vibrant self for many months, and we discovered the business had suffered; also, with an Irishman's generosity, Father gave credit and never said "No" to a hard-luck story. Now we were faced with day-books full of uncollected debts, a depleted stock of up-to-the-minute goods, and storerooms filled with old-fashioned button shoes, Christie hats, morning coats and such-like. As to the family, a younger brother and sister were still in school and two brothers were in university. Luckily my old junior room needed a supply teacher immediately, so there were three earning members of the family, but none of us on high salaries. After the funeral, before the family separated again, we talked things over. Mother said: "We're going to carry on the business. Now how shall we go about it?"

To get ready cash we had a mammoth sale. Some new stock was bought; the old stock was all brushed off, hung on racks, and bargain-priced; then we re-opened for business. For three days pandemonium reigned in our country store. Christie Stiff hats? Old-fashioned morning coats? If you got either one of them for a quarter, wasn't it a bargain! Swallow-tail coats? Just the thing for the milking barn, and two for 50 cents. Saturday night when we balanced the till, enough money had come in to pay all the oustanding bills and modestly restock the store. Incredible as it may seem, my eldest brother Bruce, before he again left for the west, had to teach both Mother and me how to make out a bank deposit slip and write a cheque.

Mother and I had always been more like sisters than mother and daughter, since I was the first girl in the family. But the two years of working closely together that followed made us good friends. My sixteen-year-old brother went in the local bank —salary, $8.00 a week. My younger sister stayed in high school. Mother ran the store during the daytime while I taught school. At nights we dressed the windows, wrote the newspaper ad for the weekly paper, entered up the books, and went out collecting. That was really tough, since debts for groceries long since eaten or shoes and stockings now worn out, are hard to face. But it did have its amusing side. One night we sallied forth with a list of people on whom to call and amounts owing, saying one to the other, "Tonight we should really bring home some cash."

The first interview shook us badly. We were kindly greeted at the door and invited in, but when the bill was presented our hospitable neighbour said: "There isn't a thing I can do about it, Mrs. Scott. The hens aren't laying and the crops weren't good. Our best cow lost her calf and potatoes are no price at all. But I would like to give you something. Just a minute." Away she rushed and came back with her deposit on the account. "Here," she said, "it's a picture of the children I had taken last week and I know you'd like to have it. Mr. Scott was so good to the children—always a bag of candies for them." What argument is there against that kind of talk? We went home and drew a line through that debt.

But even the struggle was fun. When the two boys came home from university for the week-end, they helped in the store. Saturday night was the big shopping night and the store doors were never locked until midnight. When all was quiet we would sit around the huge, pot-bellied coal-burning stove in the store and gossip. The boys would say, "Do you know what happened this week?" Mother, always a push-over for the sons, would listen intently, if not too intelligently, for her mind was on *her* news. At the first opportunity she would interject, "We got five new customers this week."

Gradually the glow of the stove would die down and half a dozen times we would say, "We must go to bed." But tomorrow was Sunday, we could sleep in, breakfast leisurely, and talk to our heart's content.

As a business investment, we decided to install a telephone. Mother, who never lost her young enthusiasm for things new, decided to put in a long-distance call to my brother Jack; and long-distance calls were not easily accomplished in those days. Finally she got him, and cried in an excited voice.

"Is that you, Jack?"

Said Jack, bewildered and upset: "What's wrong?"

"Nothing," said mother. "We've got a telephone!"

When Jack got really annoyed with Mother he would call her "Annie", a habit he'd picked up from father. So sharp and clear came over the telephone:

"Now look here Annie, don't you ever scare me like that again. I thought you were dead."

Thus ended the first long-distance call Mother put in to the boys.

And it wasn't all work. In our small village we had an outdoor rink, a Young People's Society, school concerts ,and what young moderns would call a Drama Club. We called it "putting on a play." The long rehearsals were on Friday night, and after rehearsal we went to someone's home for lunch to talk it over. This Friday night in mid-January was my night for entertaining, and since my beau was coming everything had to be perfect. I started to bake the minute I got home from school, laid the dining-room table with the best linen, the good silver, the fine china, then went off to rehearsal.

We had a combination living- and dining-room heated with a coal stove, quite elegant, with nickel knobs and mica in the doors. That night Mother decided to wash her long woollen underwear and dry it over the stove. She forgot it. When I flung open the door and said, "Come in everybody, get warm beside the stove," there it hung, the arms outspread, the legs dangling down. Things to forget? That's one of them. And the oatmeal cookies, so carefully baked, to me tasted like sawdust.

Nowadays I pick up the phone, call Western Union, and say "Take a wire please" as causually as I brush my teeth. But telegrams, when mother and I embarked on our business career, were strictly an emergency measure. One Saturday night in May Mr. Chapin, the station agent, delivered a wire which he himself had taken. Mother took it in her hand as if it were a bomb, looked at it and hesitated. "Don't worry Mrs. Scott," said Mr. Chapin, "it's good news from Bruce. He's coming home next week."

Thus fortified, Mother opened the telegram; and sure enough, there was the message. "Prepare fatted calf stop will be home Friday stop love Bruce."

Calagary and Edmonton, now oil-boom cities, were then land-boom towns with subdivisions stretching out for miles. Bruce had got in on the ground floor and had made a good profit, which he wanted to share with us. He arrived on Friday and so did the rest of the family. The "fatted calf" was on the table but we could hardly swallow for excitement; Bruce had made real folding money. After dinner he turned to Mother and said:

"Now I tell you what you're going to do, Mother. You're going to sell this whole place and you and Kate are going to take a trip out West."

Mother looked dubious. "I don't know, we're doing not badly here. Last year Katie and I took in $12,000 with this business."

"Yes," retorted her son, "but how much did you clear? How much credit are you carrying on the books?"

When she didn't want to answer a question, Mother had her own particular brand of dignity. "I don't think that's any of your business," she answered, "and anyway the trustees have raised Katie to $500 a year."

But urged by Bruce we sold the store, the house and the furniture. We went shopping for new clothes, even as far as Buffalo. Then on the first day of July we blithely embarked on a two-months carefree, all-expenses-paid holiday that took us out West on the Canadian side, and home through American cities.

Bruce made me custodian of the American Express Orders he had provided, but Mother kept a watchful eye on the expenses. She was the most illogical and lovable travelling companion with whom I've ever journeyed. We'd splurge for a week, enjoying Banff, fire-sale shopping in Vancouver, visiting ostrich farms in Los Angeles, seeing the circus in San Francisco, taking in the races at Tia Juana. Then suddenly mother would clamp down, and particularly in dining cars. The prices appalled her—50 cents for breakfast, $1.00 for lunch and $1.50 for dinner!

"We're going to have to tighten up, Katie," she'd say. "Our money's going to run out."

For a day or two we'd have a light breakfast, buy our lunch at a railway station, and have a bowl of soup at night. Then the extravagant streak would come out again and off we'd go on another bout of spending.

We met friends everywhere we went, either relatives who'd gone west or friends of my brother's. One day in the luxurious dining-room of the Alexandra Hotel we entertained a titled English friend of my brother's, Lady Anne Dartmouth. Her clipped accent (to which we were unaccustomed), her brittle sophistication, her badly concealed amusement at western ways, upset my mother. But when with the coffee she offeerd my Mother a cigarette and then lit up herself, it was the last straw. At that time North American women did not smoke in public. In the dining-room all eyes turned to view this extraordinary sight. After the departure of our guest, when Mother, badly shaken, had retired to her bedroom, she said, "I suppose Bruce must do business with people like this. But what would your father think?"

"Well," I answered, "Grandmother smoked."

"Yes," said mother, "but it was a clay pipe and not a cigarette."

It was a glorious summer and we lived it to the hilt. Every Sunday we went to church, but the rest of the week we did all the things we had read about and dreamed about and never thought would be ours. At a baseball game in Vancouver, Mother, without even knowing what "batter up" meant, rose and cheered for both sides. For the first time in her life she went to a hairdresser's, and as a crowning touch invested in pink face powder and a square of chamois with which to apply it. For us it was the Grand Tour. We came back with hearts full of memories and flat purses, and to a new home.

Chapter four

We become city dwellers

THE MOVE to Toronto seemed logical since the four older boys were already established there, and the home and business in Beeton had been sold. So in September, Peg, my younger sister, transferred to a city school, Walter was moved into a nearby bank, and I got me another teaching job at $800 a year.

The school was old-fashioned but had new equipment. Instead of working with four teachers, I was one of a staff of twenty-two. But, city or country, youngsters were just the same —irrepressible when there was mischief on foot, quiet as mice when stories of adventure were being told.

Parents, too, are the same the world over. Because I was young and new on the job they beat a path to my door. Some of them were satisfied, some dissatisfied, but all wanted to talk over the future of their children. But I was flabbergasted when an anxious mother said, "You put my Willie at the head of the class and I'll give you a nice Christmas present." Willie didn't make it and neither did I, but he did send me a Christmas card.

My room entered every school competition put forward by the Board of Education—choral class, cadet drill, and field-day games. Some of them we lost, some we won; but it was so stimulating that 9 A.M. never came early enough and 3:30 P.M. arrived too soon. To me every pupil in that room was potential material for a cabinet minister or a gifted author.

We lived in a low, rambling, cream-brick house with a large lawn in front, and at the back a well-kept garden on which the former owner had lavished loving care. Pear trees, trellis grapes

33

and espaliered peach trees, all had fruit ready for picking. During September I was tagged home from school by a dozen youngsters eager and willing to help harvest the crop—and eat it before they left.

Mother kept house for all of us and was more content than she'd been since Father died. Breakfast was rather sketchy since we all left at different times. None of us were home for lunch, but at dinner time Mother would sit at the head of the table, and with a wide smile of amusement would listen as all seven of us tried to talk at once. We're a gabby family; with even the slightest encouragement we can talk for hours. And since every one of us was engaged in different types of work, the conversation never lagged.

When we were young, Mother had always insisted that the dishes be stacked, washed, wiped and put away the minute the meal was over. But now her sons introduced a new régime, and with very clever bait. "Let's talk, Mother," they would say, "we'll do the dishes for you." Mother fell for it every time, since in this after-dinner conversation life flowed to her door.

It was a gay year. Saturday morning was given over to a co-operative cleaning of the house, with each of us responsible for our own room. But Saturday afternoon and evening the girl friends and the boy friends all gathered at our place. During the winter we danced, skated, went bob-sledding, and took in picture shows (admission price was ten cents). In the summer we played tennis, sailed, and went swimming. With half our family in school money wasn't too plentiful, but we set up a fund for Sunday treats and charged each member of the family twenty-five cents. Never did money stretch so far.

For the first time we had the experience of going to a well-organized city church with a gowned choir, ushers, and a paid organist. The minister, Mr. Geggie, the well-known one-armed Scottish Presbyterian divine, had never lost his Edinburgh burr. To his church flocked all the Scottish-born people throughout the city.

The lawns and the church hall were well equipped for all kinds of masculine sports, which was considered right and proper. But when the women sought to enter this field there was opposition from the more conservative members of the congregation. At that time gymnasium work for women and girls was just coming into vogue. When Mr. Geggie set aside one room in the church hall as a gymnasium for women, the elders of the church rose up to dispute the whole proceeding vehemently. The clerk of the session called a special meeting to fight the issue tooth and nail, and to it Mr. Geggie brought his young supporters. The elders were grouped on one side, the female gymnasts on the other, both ready to do battle. The argument waxed hotter and hotter. Finally the clerk of the session, rising to his feet and purple with indignation, shouted: "If this disgraceful thing goes through, sir, I shall leave the church."

Never one to be intimidated, and equally indignant, Mr. Geggie retorted: "If you will continue to run your factory, sir, I shall continue to run this church."

We got the gym. We bought snappy little outfits—baggy blue serge bloomers, long black stockings, running shoes, and white middy blouses. We got an instructor and we also got that modern trend—audience participation. The elders, cutting the session meetings short, sat in the gallery and watched as we went through, "one, two, three, kick, now the left leg . . . ."

It was about this time I became officially engaged to my beau, then living in Minnesota. That was in February and the wedding was set for October. In those days every bride was expected to have, as well as enough clothes to last a year, at least a dozen of everything—sheets, pillow-cases, towels, table linen. This lavish spending took every cent I had in my bank account. Mother and I carefully hemmed the linen and the boys combined forces to provide table silver and china.

As for the extras, after finishing the school year in June I supervised a playground all summer. This additional cash bought pots and pans, odds and ends.

Finally every bit of linen was monogrammed, all the preparations were complete.

The wedding took place one evening early in October, after

what could be described as "the battle of the bathtub". Every member of the family was in the wedding party—my eldest brother gave me away; Peg was one of the bridesmaids; the other four boys were ushers; the house was full of relatives . . . and we had only one bathroom! The boys said, "Kate, we've got to get to the church early so we'll have our baths first." The wedding was at eight. At seven-thirty I started running my cold tub in a bathroom littered with wet towels. But when the wedding march sounded we were all in order.

The wedding ceremony is touching and solemn, but as usual Mr. Geggie introduced his own inimitable touch. To the neighbourhood children an evening church wedding was quite an event. All my pupils and every youngster for blocks around crowded into the gallery and weren't too quiet. This upset Mr. Geggie. In the midst of "Dearly beloved we are gathered together . . . ." he glanced up, then said sternly, "Will you children in the gallery be quiet!" Dead silence, while the ceremony started all over again, "Dearly beloved . . . ."

Directly after the wedding reception my husband and I left for Virginia, Minnesota, where he had a real-estate business. This booming mining city, part of the Mesabi Range, was expanding so rapidly and business was so competitive that we delayed our honeymoon. Being young and exuberant, we made all sorts of plans. "Some day," we'd say to one another, "we'll go to Europe." But in the meantime we settled for a happy week-end late in October.

Friends of my husband had a cottage on one of the numberless lakes in that beautiful state and took us up with them Friday afternoon. Away from the open iron-ore pits that surrounded all the mining towns, Minnesota was incredibly beautiful. Here were huge forests untouched by the axe, clear lakes blue as cobalt, swift rivers teeming with fish, and stands of poplars with leaves as yellow as fresh-minted gold.

Sunday morning after the dishes were done I went for a walk, and came to an open spot where the flat outcropping of rock was warm in the sun. There, stretched out and feeling the happy melancholy that autumn always brings, I started to sing that old Kingsley song, "Oh that we two were Maying". I had just got to the last verse:

"Oh that we two were sleeping
In our graves 'neath the churchyard sod"

when my husband came looking for me. He listened, stared at me and said, "What kind of woman have I married, anyway? Do you think that's a suitable song for a honeymoon?" Henry never got used to my lyrical outbursts.

After that golden week-end we settled down to explore the country. The Mesabi Range, that famous iron-ore seam, zig-zagged upstate for miles, with lines of rail connecting every mine. Here was open-pit mining at its most rugged. Since the ore lay close to the surface, the earth was stripped off with steam shovels, then the ore was loaded into railway cars. Miners came from Italy, Hungary, Germany, Norway, Sweden, Finland —indeed, every Nordic country and all countries in central Europe had provided the labour force. They lived in such towns as Virginia, Hibbing, Eveleth, Mountain Iron, Calumet, Buhl, Biwabik and a dozen others.

The population was about 90 per cent foreign and 10 per cent Anglo-Saxon. After working hours that small minority— engineers, doctors, mine superintendents, teachers, accountants, bankers—flowed from one town to another in a never-ceasing whirl of activity and gaiety. In the winter we danced, curled, skated, skied. But more than anything else, the women played bridge incessantly up and down the Range, since help was plentiful and inexpensive.

These bridge marathons terrified me. The players were experts and my bridge was strictly amateur. After the lavish lunch (and for that feast fresh fruits, vegetables, lobster, every delicacy were brought in from Duluth) the battle was joined, with the honour of every town at stake. On one occasion the Hibbing contingent, feeling there had been dirty work at the cross-roads, swept out with fur and feathers flying. Unfortunately the argument developed an hour before the train left. But sitting in the drafty stations, they needed no fire to keep their wrath warm; it was at the boiling point.

This too was the era in which Theda Bara, the slinky voluptuous motion-picture queen, was at the height of her career. Her films, such as *The Vixen, The Vampire, The She-Devil, Serpent of the Nile, The Eternal Sin, Purgatory's Ivory Angel, Destruction, The Forbidden Path,* and *The Tiger Woman,* swept the country. When one of the Theda Bara pictures came to the Cameo picture house it was just like the opening night at the Metropolitan Opera, with everyone dressed up to the nines. The formal effect was possibly a little marred by the fact that we also had to wear heavy mackinaws, toques and fur-lined boots, since all winter the temperature stayed well below zero. But after the movie, when we all crowded into someone's home for the midnight lunch, we bloomed like pouter pigeons.

The wealth of the municipalities in this district amazed this Canadian. The mining companies paid a tax on every ton of ore mined. Half this tax went for the maintenance of schools, for paved roads, parks, hospitals, and libraries. Current rumour had it that in Hibbing, wealthiest of all the towns, half its male population was on the municipal payroll and that traffic policemen were on point duty even at lanes. Elected councils were hard put to spend their tax money. The main highways through the towns were like Great White Ways before Christmas. Every lamp post was wreathed in green, huge arches of evergreens were built from one side of the road to the other, and streets were so brilliantly lighted that the stars paled in comparison.

The schools, too, were an outlet for spending. The school population of Virginia was extremely high, and 90 per cent of the children were foreign-born or of foreign parentage. For these youngsters the most palatial schools were built, since no school board had to worry about money. Architects were imported, educational frills of all sorts were devised, and teachers were of the best. The science rooms, the shops, even the ordinary class-rooms were every teacher's dream. Just let any new educational gadget come on the market and it was in the schools before you could say "scat". My home-economics course had been taken in a school where austerity was not only preached but practised, and the lavishness of the Virginia set-up left me with my mouth open.

Demonstration housekeeping suites were set up in all the high schools, complete with immaculate white kitchens, shining bathrooms, and luxurious living quarters. Mahogany furniture, real linen, fine china, good silver, thick rugs, beautiful drapes —all were there for the education of teen-agers, many of whom at home slept four to a bed and had no rugs on the floor. Can you wonder that, dazzled by such a show of luxury, they took home anything light enough to carry? To neither the children nor their parents was this stealing; it was just making the best of a good opportunity. Scissors, thread, table silver, even cups and saucers moved out quietly and constantly.

This was a part of school life I got to know well. During the first year of our marriage I contracted smallpox, lost my first baby, and was in hospital for weeks. When I had recovered the doctor said, "Don't brood, find an outside interest." So I went back to supply teaching and not only gained a new interest in life but earned a few honest pennies with which to help pay the hospital bills.

The children of the Swedes and the Norwegians were quick and intelligent, clean and impassive. But it was the Italian children, with their warm liquid eyes and soft gentle ways, that won my heart. There were no "apples for the teacher", but when I really got in solid with the Italian children they invited me home to taste their native wine. Could hospitality go further?

And it was the Italian population who, to celebrate the discovery of America by their countryman Christopher Columbus, staged a dramatic re-enactment of this historic landing. The spot chosen was the nearby lake, with a sandy beach that lent itself to the occasion. For weeks both children and grown-ups studied pictures in the library, laboured at costumes, even built facsimiles of the *Santa Maria*, the *Nina*, and the *Pinta*, the sailing vessels with which Columbus finally reached the new world. Their research also revealed the despair of the sailors because of this seemingly endless voyage, their near-mutiny, and the implacable resolve of Columbus: "Sail on, sail on!"

Every detail was worked into the script. The props were the cane, the pole, the stick, the board, the branches covered with berries, which history records the sailors saw floating on the water as they neared land. A costumer in Duluth was commissioned to make the Columbus outfit—rich velvet doublet, long hose, even the Admiral's banner, a green cross on a white field.

Finally came the day of the pageant! The vessels stood off from the shore, the props were afloat and the excited crowds, in a holiday mood, lined the water's edge. Columbus, played by the most important member of the Italian community, strode to the bow of the ship. He shaded his eyes to sight land—and fell overboard. This was much more dramatic than the original landing. The pseudo-Columbus, fished out, dripping wet but not discouraged, again took his stance. This time the boats made shore.

That afternoon there was merriment in the streets of Virginia. Columbus was paraded up and down the main street, with a stop-over at every saloon to keep him from catching cold after his unexpected dip.

The library in Virginia was one of the many beneficiaries from the mining tax. Built of the finest materials, both inside and out, it had a collection of books, both English and foreign, that the much larger city of Duluth couldn't match. Even the children's section had fairy tales and folk-lore stories in every language. To me each daily walk downtown meant a visit to the library, and before too long the head librarian employed me to review new books and help with the Sunday-afternoon record concerts.

Records? Yes indeed. These were the days before radio and TV, when not only libraries but average families built up huge collections of records. Concerts were scheduled from two to five each Sunday afternoon. Regular attendants were permitted to request favourite operas, ballads or symphonic works. At one end of the music room a hardwood fire blazed all afternoon, burned slowly to violet ash. Around it or scattered throughout the reference room, the foreign population listened without a whisper. Every so often when the more familiar excerpts were played, a soft humming like bees in a clover field accompanied the music as a background for Caruso, Scotti, Sembrich or Schumann-Heink.

Christmas in Virginia—my first away from home—was spent

alone. Because of the serious illness of his brother, my husband was away all December, leaving me to tend the office and carry on as best I could. It was then I started making Christmas cakes for my friends and really learned cost accounting of food products. At home, when we had the store as our base of supplies, the price of raisins or currants or citron peel never entered our heads. We went into the store and took what we needed. 12 eggs or 18 eggs? It didn't matter so long as the family liked the cake. But selling a cake is a mighty different matter. You sit down to add it all up—so much for ingredients, so much for labour, so much for profit. I enjoyed it, partly because this work kept me from getting homesick. It was a happy thought that my kitchen, so far away, was just as fragrant as was my mother's kitchen.

I dreaded Christmas morning, with no one to shout "Merry Christmas!" But came one of the moments which every young wife cherishes. Before I was up the door bell rang. I rushed downstairs and was handed a flower box by the local florist. It was filled with red roses and the card said "Merry Christmas, love from your husband." Since then red roses have always been to me something really special.

My husband's only brother died that spring; so, since the flour mill was a family affair, we went back to the old home and started another life. But the Iron Range of Minnesota, the necklace of mining towns, so ugly by day, so brilliant by night, still is a vivid memory. Here was the greatest iron-ore-producing area in the whole United States. Here were unschooled, unlettered foreigners who knew music and art and appreciated them more than did the Anglo-Saxons. The pageant of autumn colour, the bitterly cold winter nights when frost wreathed the street lights like mist, the woods and the lakes, the eager response of the children, the muted music in the firelit library—that was the Mesabi Range.

Chapter five

Don't put all your eggs in one basket

B ACK HOME the honest penny was first made in poultry, and it was poultry that brought the greatest financial set-back of my life. In a night-time robbery of registered breeding stock, $6,000 vanished. Also, the thieves fired a new $1,200 breeding pen. But this disaster struck years after our return.

When we left Minnesota and returned to Canada, my husband was so busy at the mill that I had plenty of time on my hands. The house into which we moved had both a barn and a hen yard. Eggs were scarce and expensive; so, blithely and hardly knowing a pullet from a rooster, I bought a dozen pullets—White Wyandottes, because they were so beautiful with their pure white plumage, bright red combs, and yellow beaks. The farmers round about said, "Bad choice, Kate. Wyandottes are lazy and put on too much fat." I learned that they did— but not until their second year. It's the most amusing thing to see a young Wyandotte pullet, so perky and smart in her first year, gradually develop middle-age spread and adopt a leisurely type of life.

The first pullets were bought in October. Christmas day I gathered twelve eggs, one for each pullet. This was the reward of a balanced diet. These pampered beauties not only were fed grain, hot mash and green feed daily, but had fresh straw in which to scratch. They laid steadily all winter and I was able to sell eggs at a dollar a dozen. Intoxicated with this small success, I had visions of becoming a poultry farmer and bought a 26-acre farm just across the road from the family mill. On this poultry deal there was another advantage—I got my feed wholesale.

The land on the small farm was blow sand, just right for poultry. Its crowning beauty was the straight line of huge elms topping the hill. Land, buildings and equipment—that's the pattern of business; and we were into it. I paid $400 for the land. Now started the heavy financing. We had to build a house with enough room for a family of four, since now we had two small daughters. Away went another 4,000 non-existent dollars and on came a mortgage. You can't raise hens without hen pens and you can't hatch chicks without an incubator.

The first small incubator, an oil-burning contraption that held only twelve dozen eggs, was installed in the cellar. Eggs had to be turned daily and kept moist. When the first chicks began to hatch I knelt prayerfully there in front of the incubator waiting for each egg to chip, for the sodden mass to fluff out into pure gold. To me it was an epic!

For ten years we went on building, repaying one mortgage and putting on another, buying larger hatching machines, building brooder houses, until we had a flock large and selective enough to apply for official government inspection—the goal towards which we'd been working.

That fall, as soon as the range pullets were put in the pens, the Federal Government inspector arrived. Every bird was handled individually. The chassis had to be just right, the underpinning solid, because here was a real egg-laying machine. Each selected bird was banded with its own individual number, by which we recorded every egg she laid. This was made possible by the use of trap nests built in decks. When the pullet tipped the trap going into the nest, she was a captive until the egg was laid. On the huge sheets thumb-tacked to the walls of the laying pens every hen was credited with eggs laid. At the end of each week a report went into federal headquarters.

Poultry farmers are human beings—some of them not completely honest. Consequently each month the Federal Inspector came back, checked the records, handled all the birds, and knew almost to an egg whether or not those records were correct. By the shape of the body, the pliability of the bones, the receding of the color in both beak and feet, he knew! You couldn't fool these boys and we never tried.

44

It was during this ten years that I learned to respect the personality of hens. As with humans, some of them are lazy, some energetic; some are lethargic, some high-strung. Never bang a door—it puts a nervous hen off laying for days. Walk in whistling. I never could figure out whether it was the whistle or the pail of feed I carried that brought such an enthusiastic welcome. Even amongst the high-laying hens there was a behaviour pattern. The energetic biddy would wait until the last minute, hop into the trap nest, turn around two or three times, lay her egg, then bang at the trap door to be let out. The more leisurely type would saunter up to the nest two or three times, finally make it and settle down with a great clucking. Sometimes she loafed as long as an hour before producing.

The same characteristics were seen at the breakfast table. We fed the hens cafeteria style—self-feeding hoppers which were filled at night. During the winter the pen lights automatically went on with an alarm clock at 5 A.M. The busy birds were off the roost like a flash and over to the feed trough. The more leisurely type would open one eye, close it, open the other eye, have another little snooze. Then, driven by the pangs of hunger, they hopped down to look for breakfast.

The traps had to be tended every hour from 7 A.M. throughout the day. My scamper to the pens every hour on the hour wasn't conducive to steady housekeeping, but there was always the lure—will A-304 lay today? And usually she did.

It was A-304 and her daughter A-371 who established two world egg-laying records, which meant we were now in the big league. But such records were not made without co-operation on both sides. This was the day before all poultry feeds were reinforced with vitamins and minerals. Our vitamins had to be given by mouth and the minerals provided by way of green feed. The pride of our hearts—A-304—got a daily ration of crude cod-liver oil, and it *was* crude. To me, pouring it into the tablespoon, it smelled like axle grease gone high. But to my biddy it was nectar and ambrosia.

Every morning at 10 o'clock she got her special ration. When I walked in the laying pen with the demijohn of cod-liver oil and tablespoon in hand, the favourite of the flock would race like a jet plane to the jump board, fight off all intruders, down her apéritif, then rush off to consume more food. But the results more than justified the expenditure of labor.

Greens during the winter presented a greater problem. Lettuce and spinch were too expensive; cabbage by that time had bleached. So we took to green oats sprouted in the house. Our kitchen range, which had seen many curious sights, could look down in amazement at a pan of green oats, definitely out of season.

A-304, working towards a record, was pampered, spoiled and anti-social, but she did shell out the eggs. She had her own favourite trap nest on the top row, for which she battled. When the egg was laid, immediately she wanted out of the trap. Walking along the battery of nests, I would see the beady eye tight pressed against the air vent, while loud cackles demanded her release. I would open the trap and out she would hop; standing on the jump board, she was queen of all she surveyed. Waiting until I bent over the lower traps, she would land on my back just to prove that she was the most important pullet in that pen. High-production hens, just as popular movie stars, have personality and dislike moving out of the public eye.

Because of our prima donnas, many visitors came to inspect the birds before ordering baby chicks. But more important than visitors, the orders became large enough to justify installing two new electric incubators with a total capacity of 6,000 eggs.

I got busy with paper and pencil. With an estimated hatch of 80 per cent and at twenty-five cents a chick, I was sure I'd be able to meet the payments on the incubators. But it was a big investment and with little margin for error, I felt I should be right on the spot. I set up a cot in the office just over the incubator room, got so accustomed to the hum of the motors that when one night they suddenly faltered and stopped I was out of bed like a flash. I reached to switch on the light— no light! The big transformer from which we got our electric power had burned out. The steady heat so necessary for a successful hatch was cut off. I waited and hoped, but the power didn't come on soon enough. Not one chick hatched.

However, that's poultry keeping and that's life. The incubator people extended my credit and with later hatches we were able to meet our payments.

Now our stock was well known on both the North American continent and in Britain. When our largest order—for 1,000 pullets—came from the British Department of Agriculture we walked on air. Condition of the sale was that the pullets be passed and graded by both Canadian and British government inspectors.

One day late in August that inspection was completed. Every bird was perfect, every bird banded. There remained only the shipment of the pullets, after which the government cheque would be forwarded. That night I was completely happy, but had no one with whom to share my delight. My husband was off on a business trip, my two small daughters were away on holiday, and none of our help slept in. But my happiness was only a matter of hours.

Just before dawn the little beagle hound sleeping on the porch whined in such a distressed way that he wakened me. As I opened the door to let him in I saw a man running down the long lane towards the gate. With a premonition of disaster I ran to the pullet pen. The empty roosts, the sweetish, heavy odor of chloroform still hanging in the air, meant only one thing—the theft of our pullets ready for shipment.

While I pulled on a few clothes, the idling of the truck at the gate quickened to a roar and it pulled away. Our little farm truck was standing in the driveway; I jumped in and gave chase for four miles, but in my heart I knew there wasn't a hope of catching them, so I turned back. The sun was rising, but far more vivid was the blaze in the sky over what I knew was our home. My heart stopped beating; not only had the pullets been stolen but the pen fired. Freshly strawed for the inspection, it burned like tinder; nothing could have stopped the blaze.

Our village constable alerted the city police forty-eight miles away, but it was too late. In the opinion of the police the truck and the registered poultry were over the border before anyone could trace them. Stunned by the blackened ruins and my withered hopes, I walked round in a daze for a week.

47

But the honest penny was still operating in other directions; we had a young orchard beginning to bear. When we first bought our land, the agricultural experts said, "You know Kate, that south slope, with a little feeding, will be ideal land for an apple orchard—and stick to Northern Spies and MacIntoshes."

We had planted eight acres in young apple trees; and since I too was young, waiting eight years for a Mac crop and 15 years for a Spy harvest didn't worry me a particle; but in the meantime the land had to pay for itself. In between the young trees we planted buckwheat, and to enrich the soil plowed it under when it grew. After two years the land was good enough to grow early potatoes. How to get those potatoes on the market when they would bring $5.00 a bag was the problem. Again I went to the Agricultural College for advice. Early potatoes need heat for early sprouting, and by this time we had four Jersey cows in the stable, all giving off body heat. "Why not utilize that warmth?" said my advisors.

During the winter we made long wire racks and hung them from the beams over the heads of the cows. Seed potatoes were bought, cut for planting and the raw edges dusted with lamp-black to seal in the moisture. Up they went, single layers on every rack, and were left there to sprout. At first our temperamental Jerseys distrusted this overhang; but every time any of the cows tossed her head and breathed heavily upward, more potatoes sprouted. Before planting time arrived everyone in the neighbourhood had heard of this madcap adventure. "Just another example," said the experienced farmers, "of fools rushing in where angels fear to tread. Those potatoes will rot before she ever gets them planted."

They didn't rot, but sprouted beautifully. Since our soil was light and the spring unusually early, we were able to plant April 14th. It was a slow job since the potatoes couldn't be tossed in casually but had to be placed sprouts up. So, as well as the family, we had to employ six men. Need I say the planting proceeded with plenty of spectators on the sidelines giving all kinds of free advice?

It was a dull day, with heavy clouds overhead threatening rain. There was even the occasional light shower. But we

48

finished at five o'clock in the afternoon. Then occurred one of the human incidents always remembered. Said one of our small daughters, gazing skyward as the last row was covered: "Now, God, let her rain!"

The spring weather was ideal. The potatoes grew fast and so did the potato bugs; it was spray, spray all the time. But as the tops began to wither, again I indulged in my "suppositioning" book-keeping. Even at $4.00 a bag, the bank overdraft would be slimmed down.

We ordered in the potato digger, got bags and weigh scales, and started to harvest the crop. That was a big day for the village. On the hill across the road from us sat the local wise-acre with a pair of binoculars, counting the bags. We trucked the crop to market forty-eight miles away, only to find that every vegetable gardener in the more southerly part of the province was also trucking in early potatoes. Almost overnight the bottom dropped out of the market. Instead of $4.00 a bag we got 75 cents, less 12 per cent selling commission. Had it not been for the unpaid labour of the family and the Jersey cows, that transaction would have been in the red. The only black in evidence was the lamp-black, which had settled on both ceiling and walls of the stable. We had to whitewash it.

And speaking of cows, we bought our first cow so that we might have our own milk and butter for the children. I shopped entirely for looks and not for an abundant milk supply, and so ended up with a three-year-old Jersey in the stable. I had never milked a cow in my life and have never been able to decide whether that first week's milking was harder on the cow or on me. For a beginner it's quite a trick to shoot the milk straight into the pail. During that first week I would carry into the house a half pail of milk—the rest was on the stable floor, in my shoes and dripping from the bottom of my smock.

But I'd fallen in love with the gentle Jersey and planned for more. When we bought the farm we built the stable with stalls for four cows, plus a little calf pen. The first calf arrived during the night. In anticipation of this blessed event, the stall had been filled with golden-yellow straw. When I opened the stable door in the morning, there stood the proud mother; beside her

49

the tiny heifer, trying to stand erect on wobbly, outsized legs and looking so like a fawn it was hard to believe that this was our Jersey calf.

Good breeders said, "Never let her suckle the mother." So over went the baby into the calf pen. Mother and daughter were both upset by the separation; one bawled "Where is my child?" the other whimpered "Where's my food?"

If you've never taught a young calf to drink from a pail you've missed something much more exciting than the opening of the World Series. First you milk the mother—not an easy job, she's fussy. Then you take the pail of warm milk into the calf pen. To get that little head, which looks so flowerlike but is so stubborn, into the pail, to manoeuvre the mouth down to your cupped hand in the warm milk, takes strength, patience and strong language. But when this tiny heifer really learns to drink, you feel like the giver of all good and perfect things.

And here's one field, the small dairy herd, where the female of the species is more valuable than the male. The little bull-calves end up as veal, while the young heifers are cherished. They are the potential suppliers of gallons of milk, quarts of cream and pounds of butter.

Eventually, as planned, our herd was increased to four Jerseys. That meant the problem of straw, clover hay, mill feeds, and an abundance of water. We grew our own hay in the orchard, bought our straw, and got our mill feeds wholesale; but the water, piped down to the barn from the house, was icy cold during the winter. Our Jerseys turned up their noses at it, or worse still, tipped it over in the manger. So to encourage these temperamental creatures, and to increase the milk supply, we piped in warm water. That too was a neighbourhood seven-day wonder. But the investment of $10.95 more than paid off.

To the children the Jersey cows were almost a part of the family; Anne and Mary came to the stable every night when I went down to do the milking. Selfishly, this was one chore I kept for myself because I enjoyed it so much. The clean stable, the fresh straw bedding, the mow full of hay and the moos of gratitude when the mangers were filled made a symphony of contentment. The two little girls would sit on the steps in the dusk and romance to one another. They were both regular Sunday-school attendants and eagerly collected the coloured Sunday-school cards which showed Christ and His disciples in flowing robes of scarlet and purple and white. One night through the dusk I heard this dialogue.

"Look, Mary, there's Jesus up at the top of the stable."

Mary peered upward and answered, "I can't see him, Anne."

"Of course you can," retorted Anne. "See, he's got his red dress on."

Such is the imagination of childhood.

To the small daughters the little calves were much more interesting than dolls. Through that first summer when the calves weren't allowed out in the hot sun, but kept in the cool calf pen, the youngsters lugged in fresh grass, young sugar beets, every delicacy that a young heifer would enjoy. Every visitor to the farm was taken to view the little beauties and was needled into outspoken admiration. In our district we had autumn school fairs and one of our neighbours suggested to Anne that she show her favourite calf, Pansy. Then started the grooming, the increased feeding and the gentling.

On the day of the fair Pansy was brushed, her hooves were scrubbed, and she was put on a lead and proudly taken down to the fair grounds. But this temperamental calf, over-stimulated by her fellow contestants and the crowds, instead of pacing properly, took off with a flourish of heels. Flying down the show ring went Pansy, with Anne hanging on for dear life. Needless to say Pansy was disqualified, not for appearance but for show technique.

Pansy's mother, Patsy, was a roamer. It was for such types, I'm sure, that this bit of poetry was written:

> "Stone walls do not a prison make,
> Nor iron bars a cage."

Led to the pasture field, she acted as if she were riding to hounds. With one flying leap she would clear the highest fence we built; free, she would head down to the village. Then would come the inevitable telephone call:

"Mrs. A., that cow of yours is loose again. She's downtown opposite the garage."

Out would come the farm truck and the tow rope. I would drive while the girls sat in the back. Catching Patsy was a delicate, diplomatic mission; getting the rope around her neck and towing her home was an endurance test. Finally back in the pasture field, she would toss her head and give us a look which said as plainly as words: "All right, you caught me this time; but don't worry, I'll do it again." And she did.

On one of these forays, instead of heading for the village Patsy muscled her way into the feed room. A greedy creature, she ate until she could hold no more. Then she began to swell. Larger and larger bulked that stomach until I feared she would burst. A frantic call to the vet, a bottle of Blotex (giant size), and Patsy regained her figure. Can you wonder that with all these deeply personal experiences the Jerseys to us were not merely cows, they were an inexhaustible source of worry, tinged with amusement. "That Patsy," we would say, "what next will she think of?" Patsy never failed us.

You know what happens when you buy a new rug for the living-room—the furniture must be recovered, the woodwork looks a little shabby so it's a paint job, and that in turn means fresh wallpaper. This chain of circumstances was just as inevitable when we branched into the dairy business. Since we sold our cream, we had to buy a separator. That left a lot of skim-milk on hand, so we bought young pigs to use up the skim-milk. By this time, and with all the livestock and poultry, we were so busy there was no time to mow the back slope, so we bought a goat to give the lawn a crew cut. Then we discovered that churning fresh unsalted butter was more profitable than selling the cream. Off we went into another adventure, our week-end hampers for city dwellers.

Chapter six

Week-end hampers and home canning

WE HAD already worked up a Friday delivery of fresh eggs and roasting chickens to customers in the city. Occasionally, as a token of goodwill, a loaf of home-made bread, a small bowl of fresh butter, or a jar of our own red-currant jelly would be added. Our first approach for extras was made by the busy mother of five children, one of our regular customers.

"Mrs. A.", she asked, "to my order could you add a birthday cake and some cookies next week? It's Johnny's birthday—but remember, I want to pay for them."

Thus started a new and interesting business—our week-end hampers. Gradually they came to include not only eggs and a roasting chicken, but all the special treats to which a family at home looks forward. For us it meant two days' preparation each week. Bread was set Thursday night and finished Friday morning. Also on Friday we churned the butter, graded the eggs, dressed the chickens and baked. The hampers were delivered Friday night.

Word-of-mouth advertising has always been the best medium, so within a matter of months we had twelve steady customers. Containers were the easily handled egg crates. Into them went eggs, a roasting chicken, home-made bread, buns, cookies, one or two pies, a cake, jam or jelly, pickles and unsalted butter. A regular price list and order sheet was left with each customer, which meant we knew precisely what was needed for the next week-end.

Local staff was recruited for this enterprise, which was not only profitable but great fun. When the hampers were all packed and loaded in the truck, I felt like the organizer of not one but twelve highly successful parties.

Here is a wide-open field for the country woman who is a good cook, who wants to earn extra money and who can't leave home because of young children. Now let's list some pointers for this type of business.

In setting prices, allow for containers. Nowadays plastic or waxed cartons are inexpensive and suited to every need, but that cost should not be omitted.

Don't discount the cost of attractive wrapping materials. In a year's operation you'll use plenty. If your bank balance will stand the strain, buy six months' supply at a time.

Cakes light as a feather and covered with frothy icing don't journey well. Pound cakes, spice cakes or light fruit cakes, with either a dusting of icing sugar or a good solid icing, can come out of a collision or sharp turn as good as new.

Rich cookies crumble in transit. Hermits, oatmeal cookies or gingersnaps travel well. Use the same size cookie cutters all the time; set your price by weight and not by count, since the cookie batter sometimes rolls more thinly than at others. Buy broken nutmeats, which are a great deal cheaper than the whole variety.

Always draw the chickens and thoroughly cleanse and chill heart, liver, gizzard and neck; wrap in wax paper and tuck inside the bird. When delivering take a moment to show your customer how she can button-hole the incision made for dressing, which saves her sewing up the bird after stuffing. The method is simple. With a sharp paring knife make one-inch slits in the skin on each side of the vent opening, and pass these slits over the end projection of the bird. This makes a neat and easy closing.

Never, never stuff the bird before delivery. If dressing is requested, package it separately. Leave roasting instructions with each bird so that it isn't ruined in a too hot oven.

Never wash the eggs, since this removes the coating which helps to keep them fresh. If any mark needs to be removed, use steel wool. Grade the eggs carefully so that they're either extra large, large, medium or pullets. Nothing upsets a customer so

54

much as uneven grading. She thinks they should all be as big as the biggest. A special treat for the children is the coloured Easter eggs, easily done with vegetable colouring.

Pack the unsalted butter in brown earthenware pots rather than making it up in pound prints. I had a little wooden stamp made with a flower design which, pressed on top of the bowl of butter, gave it a fresh-from-the-farm look. Warn your customers that fresh butter does not keep as well as salted butter. Only one week's supply should be ordered at a time and it should be kept well refrigerated.

Never sell cream unless you have the facilities to keep it chilled during transport.

Pies, to taste really home-made, should not be lifted from the pie pan, and it's only in a proper pie pan that the bottom crust is cooked to perfection. Therefore in charting your costs add the cost of this container, which is refunded on the return of the original pie pan. You'll notice I said "original". Keep to a standard 9" deep pie pan, or even with the most honest customer you'll find yourself loaded with shallow 7" pans, which are no good for fruit pies. All our pie pans had an initialled square of adhesive tape on the bottom.

Home-made bread should be regulation size, so that sliced it fits into the toaster. Before the bread dough is shaped for the pan, weigh it to keep it standard. Rolls should be made a dozen to a pan so that the size and weight are uniform.

Before packing jams and jellies, inspect each jar carefully to see whether or not any moisture has seeped through at the sides. If so, lift off the wax and reheat in an earthenware pitcher placed in boiling water. Now with tissue blot up the moisture. Then re-apply the coating of hot wax.

Because such work is highly individual, every little gimmick you can add brings returns far beyond the money or time expended. In the autumn we always tucked in a few coloured maple leaves. For Christmas the hamper was topped with green boughs. Labels for the jams, jellies or pickles were always hand-printed and signed.

It was the preserving that took us into the field of canning on a wider scale. Most of our customers were away all summer and asked us to do their winter supply of jams, jellies and pickles. We were able to do it, since by this time we had plenty of our own home-grown products and had discovered that market gardening was a rather precarious business, located as we were so far from a major market.

The second young orchard of six acres had been set out. In between the rows and for a cash crop we had planted all varieties of fruits and vegetables—including beans.

Beans! Even yet the very thought of them makes me shudder. Our crop came into bearing just as the bottom fell out of the bean market. Worse still, on the day of our biggest picking the beans were sandy because of a heavy rain the night before. We picked, we washed, we packed and got the truck loaded. Two hundred eleven-quart baskets! Worried about the price, I called the wholesale firm with whom we dealt, and the conversation went like this:

"Hello Mr. Matthews, it's Kate Aitken here. What's the price of beans today?"

"Well," said Mr. Matthews in a hesitant tone, "not very good. How many have you got?"

"About 200 eleven-quart baskets."

"Are they washed?"

"Clean as a whistle."

"We could get 12 cents a basket—that is if they're really clean."

As I walked unhappily away from the phone, adding up costs in my little black book, I met our Irish farm hand. He took one look at my face and said, "What's the matter, missus?"

"Jim," I answered, "twelve cents a basket for those beans— that's all we're getting! The picking cost us eight cents a basket and those new baskets were eleven cents each. Then there's the planting and the hoeing and the trucking. We'll lose at least twenty cents a basket on that load."

Jim clucked sympathetically, then gave with this pearl of wisdom. "Too bad, missus. But it just goes to show you what I keep telling you. It doesn't pay to keep books."

From that time on the bean crop went into pickled-bean relish, on which there was a profit.

By this time we were growing such fruits as strawberries, raspberries, red and black currants, and gooseberries. On the vegetable side, besides beans (perish the thought!) we had tomatoes, cucumbers, cauliflower, peppers, onions. As our canning business grew in volume, most of the products grown on the farm were pickled, jammed, jellied or otherwise preserved, and were sold to private customers or to exclusive food stores.

The home canning enterprise started modestly. I bought two five-burner oil stoves, two wash boilers, glass jars by the gross, and sugar in hundred-pound lots. All the work was done in the big, cool basement of the house, with equipment and staff added as the demand for our products grew.

The oil stoves sat side by side on a platform beside the deep double sinks, which also served as laundry tubs. Next to the stoves were long wooden tables on trestles for the filling of the jars or glasses when cooking was completed. On the far side of the basement were the preparation tables, and here sat our staff, a small United Nations group. We had Canadians, English, Irish, Scottish, a German wayfarer, and a Pennsylvania Dutch helper. But as well, since most of them were married and couldn't come to work without the young children, we had a kindergarten—and that was the real problem.

To keep the youngsters out of the basement, entertainment and food had to be provided. Hence the back lawn was littered with doll carriages, wagons, shovels—every kind of toy imaginable. In self defence we built a play house, which also served as a woodpile. We already had the wood, since to circumvent Patsy, our roaming Jersey, and her offspring we had torn down the old cedar fence and put up a cow-proof wire fence. The cedar posts were sawed into stove lengths, then piled to form a hollow square with an opening at the front. To make it rainproof it was covered with long cedar rails. There the children played happily for hours on end. But we still had to keep a watchful eye on them. Obsessed with the canning operations, the children built their own stove from old tin cans, begged old jars, and started their own canning industry. After the first blaze we suggested cold-water canning.

Then there was the problem of discipline. Some of the little boys had picked up quite a vocabulary, duly copied by the little girls. On all of them, my own and the neighbours', I tried the "wash-your-mouth-with-soap" technique, only to have further trouble on my hands. The children didn't object, but you should have heard their anguished mothers.

Every day it was a three-ring circus, which started at 8 A.M., rose in a crescendo at high noon, and finally abated at 6 P.M. when everyone went home. In the gardens the pickers gathered for us the fruits and vegetables. What we needed for canning orders was in the jars the same day; any surplus was loaded in the farm truck, which I drove down to the city fruit market that night. And this to me was the most peaceful part of the day. Traffic wasn't too heavy, there were no decisions to make, no telephone to answer, no disputes to arbitrate, no children to discipline. Even the fruit market was quiet, with only the night watchman, who spoke broken English, to check in the supplies.

The little farm truck, always overloaded, took quite a beating. The engine would heat up, the tires got worn and the necessities of my life included learning how to baby the engine, and how to change a flat tire on a lonely country road at midnight. Surely you remember those old trucks, with everything in the most inconvenient places. All the tools were under the front seat and the spare tire was set against the back of the cab.

As I was coming home one bright moonlit night with a load of glass jars, WHOOSH! went one of the rear tires. There was nothing to do but change it, so I climbed out, unloaded the truck, got out the spare tire and the jack, and went to work. At that point along came a farmer in a buggy. He pulled up and called out very kindly, "In trouble missus?"

"Yes," I answered, "I've got a flat tire."

He sat there comfortably in the buggy—all 250 pounds of him—watched me jack up the truck and take off the tire. Then he called, "Well, good luck!"—and drove on. Fury lent speed to my efforts; never was a tire changed so quickly or so bitterly.

But no matter how late the hour when I arrived home, there was one pilgrimage I always made—down to the basement. Since the orders for private families covered the whole season, these were not delivered until October, when the order was completed. As the work progressed the jars were stored on long shelves, bunked off for each family and with the name above each section. I would turn on every light, walk over and gaze happily at that rainbow of color—crimson jelly, golden peaches, dark red berries, tiny green tomatoes. Yes, even the bean relish now could thrill me.

Every season of the year, driving in the gateway at home was the best part of going away. In the fall, after the apple orchard came into bearing, there was the fragrance of the MacIntosh apples, sweeter than a rose garden. After the snow came, the bare black branches of the trees stood out like an India-ink etching on a white ground. In springtime, when the orchard was in bloom, there was all the promise of a bountiful harvest. The driveway was lined with daffodils; at night their tall golden trumpets marked the way. With summer came the smell of the ripening fruit, the sharper note of freshly cut grass. At all times of the year, and particularly at night, the little farm seemed a quiet haven. It was my world.

Feeding the staff with their children was one of the major problems; and we were always able to get pickers and canning staff, because the word had gone abroad that we fed them well. Sharp at half past nine the canning staff laid off to make jam sandwiches and pots of tea. When the whistle blew everyone came running and the food melted like snow in a January thaw. The picking staff went home for noon dinner, but the canning staff stayed for the hot meal—meat, vegetables, pickles, fruit, tea, hot biscuits; the oven was never cold. We bought beef by the quarter, hogs by the carcass, flour by the hundredweight and shortening by the keg. Again at half past three came the afternoon snack—more jam sandwiches, and if the picking had been good, fresh cakes. The staff ate a large proportion of the profits, but gave it back in good work. One of the lessons I learned was this; workers, like an army, travel on their stomachs.

With a highly diversified group of workers such as we had, whose ages ranged from eighteen to seventy, naturally there was a clash of personalities. You wouldn't imagine that a thirty-five-cent paring knife would lead to deception and bad temper, but that's actually what happened. The knives were exactly alike—but not to the staff. Each woman had her own favourite paring knife and wouldn't work with any other. First of all they tried scratching their initials on their knives, but the scratches didn't go deep enough. Then we entered on the period when, after the night wash-up, the paring knives were carefully hidden under the tables, behind jars, and finally in the furnace. But at 8 A.M. every knife came out of its hiding place.

Then there was the battle of food. The two spinster sisters started coming at 7:30 after their milking was done, and quietly prepared for themselves a lavish breakfast. What could you say? Nothing, just enter it up on the debit side of the books. There was a constant clash as to who should wash up the dinner and tea dishes. This controversy became so acute and nerves so high-strung, we finally settled it with everyone washing not only her own dishes but her children's. (I was left with the pots and pans.)

Since chopping vegetables, skinning peaches, stemming strawberries and such-like employed the hands but not the head, there was gossip, gossip all day long. With us was Mary, a young red-headed school-teacher, newly graduated from teachers' college and looking for a job. This was during depression, when there were ten school-teachers for every available position. One day in August Mary's father drove up to the back door and shouted for her. Out she rushed, talked confidentially to her father, and came back into the basement like a Christmas candle all lit up. Although we all looked at her expectantly, not a word of news did she give. When she left one of the spinster sisters turned to the other and asked, "Did Mary get her job?"

"I don't know, she didn't tell us and I didn't like to ask her."

Deep silence and a lot of pondering while the paring knives slowed up. "Well," said the sister, "what you could have said was 'I hear teaching jobs are scarce this year'; then you would have found out."

Because most of our clients were socialites who spent the

summer away from the city, and since most of their names were well known to the members of our staff, they were intensely interested in the customers. "My, oh my," they would say as we packed up a full load, "these people must have lots of money. How many jars did they order? What kind of house do they live in?" And then the final question, "Do they have a butler? Does he wear a swallow-tail coat?" It was a case of reflected glory. For any family with a butler the jars got a special shine in deference to the swallow-tail.

For the pickers, who came early but couldn't start picking until the dew was off, we bought two croquet sets. From a simple, harmless game it developed into a betting arena.

Pickers were paid by the crate and they all needed the money. But in the passionate heat of this croquet tournament they would wager their whole day's picking. In the interests of family finance we packed up the croquet sets.

Inevitably some rows of fruit are better than others, and here again we ran into controversy. One of our pickers brought along her whole family. When the day's picking ended, she would collect crates and boxes for the next day, leave them at the end of the best rows farthest from the house, and next morning start her family picking without checking in. Cries of "unfair practices" came from the other pickers when they realized what was going on. So I walked down to the family group to lay down the law.

"A situation such as this breeds discontent," I said. "The rows must be picked one by one in rotation."

"That's right, Mrs. A.," said the mother self-righteously, "that's what we've been doing."

I turned up the next row, thinking the whole affair had been settled, and by now I was completely hidden by the tall berry bushes. Piped one of the youngsters to his mother, "Mummy, what does Mrs. A. do?"

In a deep, positive voice came the answer, "Nothing much, Andy, just sort of dandies about upsetting us."

It was this same family who systematically hijacked one box out of every twelve picked. Casually one of the youngsters would saunter to the fence separating our property from the community park and hide them. That night the berries were sold to our grocer. However, we never went into this very closely, since the whole family picked so well and with such clean precision that I figured it wasn't worth losing their expert help.

But the rigours of picking were frequently offset by the drama of our daily life. My husband, a dog fancier, bred and sold registered beagle hounds. When he was away on business the feeding of the young pups was part of our daily work. One lovely summer day I decided to oil and grease the truck, and was just in the middle of this messy chore when a cry for help came from the basement. I left the can of grease sitting by the truck. The pups, frolicking around the yard, attacked it with the most passionate abandon. When I returned to finish the job every pup was sick. We called the vet and up he came, equipped with a stomach pump.

This was too good a show to miss; pickers, canners and youngsters crowded round to see the show. One after one, after being pumped, the limp little forms were laid on straw. Prayers went up for their recovery. Fortunately for me they all lived. And such was the loyalty of the workers that not one word of this terrible episode was ever breathed to my husband. The vet took his pay in raspberries, after which the whole ghastly business was a closed book.

As well as drama, every day brought something amusing. When we served fresh cake the spinster sisters would carefully remove two pieces each, wrap up the extra slices and say, "We're not very hungry now, we'll take these home for supper."

To save laundry our whole group wore khaki outfits—blouses, bloomers and button-on skirts. A newspaper reporter, coming out one day to do a story about our enterprise, looked at all these khaki-clad figures and exclaimed, "What is this, a summer camp?"

Then there was the English client who ordered four dozen jars of pickled green tomatoes, the tiny ones. When I delivered them he said, "My wife and I so enjoy these with our breakfast toast." It amused but didn't disturb me. Some people like these pickles with toast, some with cold meat. All I was interested in was the order.

Every morning the oil-burning stoves had to be cleaned and the oil containers filled. No one wanted to do this job so we had to set up a regular schedule. When Kitty was late we knew it was her stove-cleaning morning and that her late appearance was carefully calculated.

Good jam needs constant skimming, and the skimmings we threw out. But one day our English girl asked, "Do you mind if I take all the skimmings home? That's the way my Ernie likes his jam."

But the arrival of the baby carriage capped everything. One member of our staff, who was "expecting", wanted a baby carriage. She asked me to buy it for her and keep the cost out of her pay. "Don't mention it to any one," she said. So I didn't. But the afternoon the express man delivered the baby carriage, the word went round the village like wild-fire. "Another baby on the way up the hill, and Mrs. A. so skinny."

Although we had no unions in our small village and portal-to-portal pay was unknown, we never expected extra work without extra pay. One of the specialty shops we supplied phoned one morning to ask, "How quickly can you get in another hundred jars of red-currant jelly?"

"By tomorrow," I said, and then started figuring. Our own yield of red currants didn't run to this additional order, which meant an immediate journey to the wholesale market. (For red-currant jelly to be at its best, currants have to be picked, stemmed, cooked and strained all in one day.)

At five in the afternoon the red currants and myself arrived home. I said, "Can any of you girls stay late tonight?"

The working wives all answered, "Can't be done. Bill (or Jim or Tom, whoever the husband might be) has got to have his hot supper."

However, the two spinsters volunteered, and after a hearty meal went to work. The stemming was done by 9 P.M., the cooked red currants straining in their flannel bags by 10 o'clock. Before I could enter up the payroll, said one spinster to the other: "I've always heard that work after six o'clock was time

63

and a half, haven't you Rebecca?" So it was time and a half, with a full-course supper thrown in. But the order was worth it. Every job has its perquisites. Most office workers take home pencils, scratch pads, elastic bands and paper clips and think nothing of it. With our canning staff it wasn't paper clips, but eggs. In order to revitalize the breeding stock, we let the hens run freely on range after six months' heavy egg laying. With the brisker hens the recuperative period was short. Then, filled with enthusiasm and reverting to type, they began laying in the far-off corners of the farm. With pickers or canning staff it was "finders keepers". We never delved into that operation.

Odds and ends of jam, half jars of pickles, left-over fruit or vegetables—to me it seemed better to give it away than have it quietly abstracted when my back was turned.

Because we were on a six-day week and a ten-hour day, the household laundry had to be slotted in just wherever we could make time for it. We had six beds on the go, which meant plenty of sheets and pillow-cases. There were work clothes, Sunday clothes, play clothes, and dozens of tea towels and bath towels, which all added up to laundry every other day. Away went good hard cash for an electric washing machine and mangle. Did any one of our staff object to washing or ironing? Not a bit, with this electrical equipment. But suddenly I noticed on the clothes line garments that didn't belong to us at all. Staff workers, short of time at home, just brought along their own laundry and ran it through with ours. To that also I turned an unseeing eye.

Is there still a market for such expensive, personalized food products? Very definitely; and nowadays, with modern equipment, the work could be done with half the labour. But to offset this advantage, labour, oil, electricity, containers, equipment and raw products have trebled in price. Happily, though, there still remains the type of gourmet who will pay the price in order to get delicacies that taste like the ones Mother made.

For those of you who would like to earn an honest penny in this highly specialized market, here are the essentials:

Freshly picked fruits and vegetables should always be used, then the finished product is Grade A.

Carefully cost-account every item in the the process of manufacture. This includes production, *i.e.*, cost of fertilizer, seed, planting, cultivation and picking. Preparation labour for fruit and vegetables should be costed separately, as should containers. One very popular pickle we made, Queen's Mustard Pickle, was an outstanding example. Ingredients for a pint jar cost 4½ cents; preparation of the six ingredients cost 13 cents, almost treble the cost of the ingredients themselves; containers cost 9 cents. This was the most costly pickle we produced, but the best seller.

Since time of boiling, etc. varies with every product, the most reasonable method is to keep books for the entire season, then apportion so much fuel cost to every jar.

Second-hand jars are never an economy when selling a high-quality product. Neither should jar rubbers be used a second time. Keep to uniform containers, which make for easier ordering and packing and for customer satisfaction. Never destroy the cartons in which the containers are received. You'll need them for packing and delivering the filled jars.

See that labels are always placed in the same position, are unwrinkled and straight. Labels should be placed one-third of the way down the jar so that they are always visible.

Start selling in a small way, preferably with a well-placed specialty shop in a good district.

Never deliver a container that is not absolutely perfect and immaculately clean.

Label each carton with the contents, the name and address of the customer, and the number of cartons in the order. Chart your delivery route so that no time is wasted in city traffic. Pick up canning supplies for the return trip so that the car is loaded both going and coming.

Transport should include not only the cost of gas and oil but the general upkeep of the car or truck. After 50,000 miles, repair bills are so heavy that a new vehicle is an economy. But unless in your budget a certain sum of money has been set aside each year for the new vehicle, you'll find yourself with a whopping big bill and monthly payments that you can't afford.

On the homeward journey stop at a quiet restaurant, there to relax with food and a hot beverage. And if you want to completely wipe out your own problems, casually enquire of the proprietor, "How's business?" You'll drive home quite certain that you are one of the lucky people in the world.

It's hard work but fun. Turning out 12,000 jars a year from a small home canning plant as we did, means a real production line. To personalize our products, the label on every jar was hand-printed and signed "Kate Aitken". One September day I delivered a shipment to one of the specialty shops that we supplied, and quite properly the delivery was made to the service door. Mr. Barron, head of the establishment, said, "Kate, have you seen the front window? Come and have a look."

There, tier on tier and filling the whole window, were the fruits of our labour, with a huge sign that read "Kate Aitken's Home-Made Specialties". Almost, but not quite, I forgot to collect the cheque.

Chicken in glass, we discovered, was much more profitable than a non-laying hen on the hoof. Our White Wyandottes, chosen because of their handsome appearance, were truly beautiful. The snow-white feathers, the bright yellow of beak and feet, the Chinese-red comb created a spectacular effect. Stepping about in the pullet year, these slim, suave, well-groomed beauties looked like fashion models on a feathered runway— and that first year they really produced. But in the second year, except in rare cases, they would loaf and nibble all day, thus developing middle-age spread. Down would go the egg production and up would come the weight. For years we took the easiest way out, sold our fat hens, the non-paying boarders, to the Jewish market, which gave me one of my most amusing stories.

Two of our Jewish buyers, Abie and Benny, became great friends of ours, were always welcome at the farm and kept closely in touch with my travelling to and fro. One fall, when I had just returned from a six weeks' trip to Europe on a government assignment, I was not surprised to see the familiar truck turn in at the gate. On this particular journey I had enjoyed the unusual experience of an interview with Mussolini, then the dictator of Italy. Because of his unique position and the fact that I was a woman, this interview had received considerable play in the newspapers—a fact well known to Abie. That morning, clad in overalls and shirts, we were bringing in the pullets off the range and placing them in the pens.

The truck pulled up and Abie rushed forward with outstretched hand. With him, instead of Benny, was his young nephew Morris, who'd never been to the farm before. All in one breath, and pumping my hand up and down, Abie said, "Morris this is Mrs. A., have you any nice fat hens? Ah you're a sight for sore eyes!"

Morris, quite unimpressed, eyed me up and down as if I were one of the denizens of Tobacco Road. To his way of thinking, respectable woman didn't wear overalls. Abie was quite upset, turned to his nephew and said, "Morris, you don't understand, this is Mrs. A., you seen her picture in the papers, she fly the Alps, she see Mussolini."

Morris looked at me in amazement, then gave forth with this comment: "*She* fly the Alps? *She* see Mussolini? Well, you never can tell from the looks where the brains is."

That contract with my Jewish friends lasted for two years. But in the meantime we had started canning the fat hens for our own table use. Since our poultry plant was under government inspection and somewhat of a show-place, we never knew when visitors would arrive, and a ready-cooked chicken dinner was a handy ace in the hole. Done in glass, the hens looked so attractive that we began putting them in our week-end hampers as Christmas gifts. Then the orders flocked in, not only from private families but from Miss Sutton's Tea Room, one of the better restaurants. An American visitor, dining at Miss Sutton's, was intrigued with her display of our canned chicken; and that in turn led to a sizeable order from a restaurant on the Boston Post Road. We were now launched on hen canning, quite a project, and were quite proud of the fact that our products were selling in two countries.

Following on the heels of the last pickling, the new venture also meant additional work for our local staff. First catch your hen—that was the initial step in this project. Loafers were separated from the workers at night when the birds were roosting. It was an easy process. The pelvic bones of the laying hens are thin and flexible, of the non-layers firm and close. Candidates for the glass jars were segregated and starved for 24 hours to empty the crop.

Then came the chore that I always dreaded—the killing. Experts at the agricultural college claimed that sticking the birds was far more effective than chopping off their heads. So I took a day at the college to learn the technique of sticking. After minute instruction I was handed two birds and a sticking-knife. I tried it and fainted. That was enough for me. After that I stayed with the chopping block and the axe. On those mornings there was always a gallery of children. As they sat on the ridge pole of the hen pen to view the mass execution, I envied them their blithe acceptance of the natural end of a lazy hen.

Once this unpleasant work was completed we went into an assembly line. The birds were first dipped in boiling water so that the feathers could be easily removed, then cut into serving pieces and simmered till tender.

Canned chicken, to look its best, should be in a firm, clear jelly; early in the game we discovered that the feet, scaled and skinned, then cooked with the joints, ensured the jelly content. The meat was never taken off the bones, since that sweet flavour was needed. The tender joints were packed in quart jars with the white meat on one side the dark meat on the other. The stock was strained, the jars filled to within a quarter-inch of the top. After the tops and rubbers were lightly adjusted the jars were processed for two hours in boiling water. Later we discovered that all-white meat for chicken salads was another best seller; the dark meat we canned for chicken pot pies. We also found that recipes for the preparation of either chicken pot pies or chicken salad made a welcome addition to the pack. These receipes were fastened to each jar.

68

A five-pound bird will adequately fill a quart jar, and for these we were paid $2.00. Sold live, these boiling hens netted us between eighty and ninety cents each. Even with the cost of the jars, labour, trucking and labelling, we made a profit of fifty cents a jar.

From this experiment, as well as from our experience with fruits and vegetables, one important lesson was learned—the farther you get from the raw product, the greater the margin of profit. So it is that pickles are more profitable than raw vegetables, cakes and cookies more profitable than eggs, canned chicken more profitable than boiling hens.

The canning was going well, so too were the hampers and the jellied chicken. These were strictly feminine ventures in which my husband shared only vicariously, since managing the mill was a full-time job. But for the next honest penny we moved into a man's world.

Chapter seven

A man and his dog — and others

"A MAN and his dog"—that's a phrase as old as time. One of the most lovable traits that Henry possessed was his devotion to dogs—any dog, large or small, so long as it was a thoroughbred. Moving about the country as we did after our marriage, it was impossible to keep a dog. But when we settled in to the family mill and a permanent home the first investment was a pup. My enthusiasm was only lukewarm. At this time the mill went into around-the-clock operation and Anne, our first baby, was born. Since Henry's hours were so uncertain he felt I needed a dog for protection. What argument could I put up?

So we bought an Airedale. Dog propaganda flew around our house like confetti after a wedding. Airedales, I was told, are the most devoted canines that ever walked on four feet. "A one-master dog," my husband assured me. Timmy, our Airedale, went farther than that. He became a one-baby dog and neither slumbered nor slept. In the day-time when the carriage was outside he lay beside it and ferociously barked at every delivery boy. At night he insisted on sleeping beside the crib of this red-headed mite, and at the slightest outside noise he growled. It got to the point where I could get no groceries or milk delivered, since everyone was afraid of this protector by day and by night. Timmy was sold.

Shortly afterwards we bought our small farm and went into chickens. Said my husband, "What we need around this place is a good watch-dog." So we bought a great Dane. He was huge, and he ate more than a horse. Then for an extra tidbit he would snaffle off three or four pullets. The air was rent with the wild squawks of the biddies as he chased them from pillar to post.

A watch-dog, locked up, is useless, so we evolved "the system of the clothesline". By day his long chain was looped to the clothesline and he tore up and down like a wild thing. When this amusement palled he dug huge holes up and down the line of march. They looked like craters and felt like them when the unwary fell into them. When the laundry went on the line we had to shut him up in the barn. He learned to unlock the doors.

One day I had just finished packing a thirty-dozen crate of eggs for shipment and had walked up from the basement to the kitchen. Five minutes later noises below were a little suspicious, and I went down to investigate. It was a crate disaster. Never have I seen a messier-looking uncooked omelet. There were egg shells all round and dozens of raw eggs had been swallowed or just broken.

But when this inveterate seeker after food took to chasing the farmers' sheep it was the end, since good customer relations with the local farmers dealing at the mill couldn't be imperiled. Rex, too, was sold.

Undiscouraged, my husband was still looking for a dog that would fit into our way of life. Night after night he would study breeders' catalogues; then finally he hit on this idea: we would buy a beagle hound—kind, gentle, easily fed, and small.

When the first beagle arrived in her small travelling crate the children could hardly believe their eyes—she looked like a toy. Before a week had passed, she had won all our hearts with her gentle ways. Long before breeding time arrived, the prospective father had already been selected. Naturally he was pedigreed, but also he had to stand no higher than fifteen inches, and must have a smooth white coat with large patches of black and tan suitably interspersed. He had to be sound of wind and limb and enjoy hunting rabbits.

When Jasmine left home we were all lonely. When she returned she was given the utmost care. Our expectant mother was bedded down in the softest straw, fed a balanced diet, and exercised regularly. When the tiny pups arrived, excitement round our house ran high. They were so little that each one could be held on the palm of the hand. And there were six of them—four males and two females.

To my amazement, I discovered that there is an honest penny in beagle pups. It's a popular breed, not only because of the size, but also because the soft brown eyes and the long drooping ears are a definite bid for love. Then too, a beagle around the house is neat, tidy and as companionable as an old shoe. Once advertised the little creatures sold immediately to all sorts of people. One letter, which came from a station agent in the far north, was so amusing I still have it. In part it read, "This is a lonely part of the country and my wife and I would like a beagle for company. We have been married a year and have not a pup yet."

The first accouchement was successful—the second was not so happy. Unfortunately Jasmine was killed two days after the litter (again of six) was born. My husband felt that a litter as large as this was too young to rear by hand and decided they should be done away with. No one had the heart to drown them, indeed we were all in tears. Said my husband, "It must be painless," and decided on carbon monoxide from the car exhaust. The dreaded operation over, he went into the garage to bury the little fellows, only to find one of them still alive. He brought it up to the house and from that time on Sammy, as we called her, ruled the roost. We phoned the vet to see what and how to feed her. He gave us the right formula and advised us to use a medicine dropper. Feedings every two hours were the order of the day, with this tiny creature curled up in the hand and swallowing greedily every sweet drop of skim milk and brown sugar.

House-reared, Sammy looked on every room as her particular domain. Early in the morning she rose from her basket, and came scratching at the bedroom door, imploring, "Let me in, let me in." It was easier to hop out of bed and let her in than listen to that plaintive appeal. When the door opened she would dart past me like a streak and take a flying leap into my warm spot in the bed, leaving the cold side of the sheet for me. But as a foot-warmer she was better than an electric pad. She would burrow to the bottom of the bed, and what she used for oxygen we never discovered.

This close companionship was on one occasion too intimate for comfort. Sammy, an inveterate rabbit hunter, on one of her midnight forays tangled with a skunk. This time she was let in by the front door, and as usual headed straight for the bed. Followed a lengthy process which involved a tomato-juice bath for Sammy, a complete change of bedding, and de-skunking the mattress.

Like all dogs, Sammy loved riding in the car, and it was quite a trick to get down to the village without her. If I by-passed her she headed straight for the post office downtown, where she knew I could call. There she would stand, wagging her tail and waiting to ride home in triumph.

Good diet and exercise are what give the beagle its smooth, glossy coat and shining eyes, so my husband started to experiment with all kinds of dog feed. He tried out molasses, cod-liver oil, bone meal, pulverized meat, fish meal—every possible combination for health and vigour; and their preparation turned our kitchen into a lab. All these mixtures smelled to high heaven, so we kept them in a series of tin cans on the shelves leading down cellar. And now happened an incident that even to this day is not a joke.

My husband loved hot porridge for his supper and knew exactly how he wanted it made. The oatmeal should be poured into rapidly boiling water, with just enough salt; then cooking should be long and slow. On this particular Saturday night our two small daughters and I had gone down to a church supper, leaving Kitty, who helped us by the day, in charge. The last thing I said as I walked out the door was, "Kitty, now you will be careful about the porridge, won't you?"

We came home to find the contents of the double boiler untouched and the whole house smelling like rancid fish meal. Unknowingly Kitty had cooked up a large batch of the latest issue of dog mix and then departed, feeling she had carried out instructions to the letter.

Bathing Sammy was reserved for Sunday morning, a chore usually done in the kennels or the barn. But properly spoiled

Sammy was done in the house bathtub, with our two daughters eager onlookers. This procedure always stretched my devotion a little thin, so while the bath proceeded I dust-mopped the house with more abandon than was necessary. "Wooden curses", my mother used to call such conduct. But worse was in store! Sammy escaping from the biggest, best bath-towel, rushed out into the living-room, and shook herself vigorously beside the piano. "Get out!" I said, swinging the dustmop in Sammy's general direction. She fled, howling. My husband did nothing to ease the situation by taking the dustmop from my hands and saying reproachfully, "Now you've hurt her feelings."

Dog lovers know no bounds to their affection, and my husband was no exception. One lovely autumn Sunday I said, "Let's pack a lunch and drive up to Hockley Valley. It would do us all good." But when, equipped with lunch hampers, I walked out to the car, Sammy and her new pups were in the back all ready for the day's outing. I said to my husband, "The pups are rather young, aren't they? They might get car-sick."

"Oh no they won't," he answered. "A day's outing will do them good too."

The road to the valley is narrow and winding. The hills are steep and the curves are sharp—and the worst happened. Every pup was car-sick. Very selfishly I walked away to look at the view, leaving the clean-up job to the dogs' owner.

Did we make money out of beagles? Yes, we did. But they also paid a dividend in love and affection, in joy and happiness. If you have a beagle in the house no welcome mat is needed at the door. When you come home at night, it warms your heart when that neat little creature stretches, yawns, then comes over to rub her head lovingly against your knee. In effect she's saying, "Gee, missus, I'm glad you're back; and see, I waited up for you."

But if you should happen to meet up with a beagle enthusiast, discount some of the fabulous tales he tells you. To this day, and in spite of evidence to the contrary, my husband claims that when he took down his fishing-rod, Sammy went over behind the woodpile and began to dig for worms.

Henry also insisted that beagles understood every word that

75

was spoken to them—indeed, were far smarter than many humans. But our old gray cat could outsmart the beagles every day in the week. The local slaughter-house was located in a tiny field about half a mile from the farm. The butcher very kindly would toss out bones for the beagles—a treat they thoroughly enjoyed. But the cat, equipped with her own Distant Early Warning system, would establish herself on the gate-post to await their return. Then, as the beagles rushed through the gate with these juicy bones firmly clamped in their jaws, she would drop on top of them. Startled, they dropped their bones and she salvaged these delicacies for herself. Once well fed she took their morning toilet in hand. Purring with delight, while the beagles sat quiet as mice in silent ecstasy, she would wash their faces from ear to ear.

Our goat, christened Nellie by the children, all summer had done a mammoth job on the back slope. Tethered each day, she cleaned the grass off like a low-set power mower. To amuse themselves and Nellie, the children would lead her round the yard, even with the knowledge that these journeys would be interrupted by a good sharp bunt from the rear. By October Nellie was part of the family, but we had no place to house her through the winter, since the barn was filled to capacity. So one morning I called our butcher to ask him if he could despatch Nellie and prepare her for the table. Unfortunately, the children saw her led away and also saw her coming home, neatly wrapped in brown paper.

The Sunday roast was succulent, crisp on the outside and tender on the inside, and it carved beautifully. But the children took one look at it, then asked, "Is this Nellie?" Not one mouthful would they eat. Fortunately the canning staff was not so sentimental, and enjoyed Nellie to the last tasty mouthful.

How many times have you joined in chorusing the diversity of Old Macdonald's livestock? By the time we added six young pigs to our menagerie I knew exactly how he felt. But conditions seemed ripe for including pigs in our farm population. The price of pork was good. With four cows in the barn, we had plenty of skim-milk. Also we had enough cedar rails left to build an outdoor pigpen; and since this was a summer proposition, all the pen needed was a partial shelter.

After enquiring around, we located the pigs at a farm about four miles away. The farmer was willing to part with them, but the young piglets had their own ideas about leaving home. Our first trick was to catch them. Not only were they as slippery as eels, but the squealing was really nerve-racking. At last they were caught, bagged and put in the back of the truck. All the way home the squealing continued—it sounded so human, I feared we might be stopped for kidnapping.

Fortunately the children never developed the deep affection for the pigs that they had so freely given Nellie the goat. Every feeding time was a pitched battle. But the little piglets grew into fine big porkers and more than paid for their board and keep.

None of us liked the pigs—no personality there. Just six yawning caverns to be filled, fattened and taken to market. It was with the greatest relief we ripped down the pigpen, cleaned it up, and cashed the cheque.

Possibly you may feel the same, reading this chronicle of chores and cleaning, of pigs and goats, as did my mother. Visiting us periodically, she became slightly confused with the beehive of activity in which we were engaged. Sometimes, laying down her knitting, she would say, "You know Kate, just to watch you makes me tired." But to us it was vibrant living. Although our main preoccupation was paying for the farm and meeting the bills, life was never dull.

One of the pleasant occupations in which the whole family participated was the growing, gathering and garnishing of gourds, which we sold as Christmas gifts. All we needed to do was plant the seed, give the gourds plenty of growing space, and leave them alone.

We gathered them in the fall—all shapes and sizes, each one as individual as a musician. First of all they had to be dried, and to promote adequate drying two small holes were bored in the neck of the gourd. Then, well protected, they were left on top of the furnace until the inside pulp had lost all its moisture.

77

On forays to the woods we gathered milkweed pods that had split open, and pine cones.

The first week in December the cans of enamel and the little paint brushes came out. Everything—gourds, pine cones, milkweed pods—was enamelled in lovely shades of rose and red, apple green and blue, pale chartreause and daffodil yellow. Strung on raffia, these mementoes of the outdoors not only made fireplace ornaments, but could be used to fill a large wooden bowl, a table centrepiece. They were so lovely we hated to part with them, but Christmas sales were good.

Did we have any social life? It never stopped. Indeed, sometimes I wondered how we got our work done, since every night was so crowded. In the midst of our baking we were constantly being phoned: "Could you make a chocolate cake for the bridge tournament next Thursday?" or "We have you down for two loaves of sandwiches for the Community Concert. If you can't come, be sure to send the sandwiches. We need them." Among ourselves we had an abundance of entertainment—bridge parties, dances, ice carnivals, and amateur theatricals.

At the mixed bridge club at night, when the men were present, we were all on our best behaviour and played a conventional game. But during the afternoon sessions, when the women were on their own, attention was apt to stray and conversation flourished.

But as well as social life we aimed at culture. Our library, which was situated behind the post office, was well equipped with good books—but closed promptly at five in the afternoon. We needed a club-room for the young men and women of the community, some place where they might meet one another. So the library, with its gaily coloured book jackets and shaded lights, was opened at night and staffed by the women's committee. What did it matter if, instead of taking down from the shelves *The Adventures of Captain Scott,* the young readers brought in their own copies of current magazines and used them as a cover for shy love-making?

For the older and more settled members of our wide-spread community, the services of the nearest university were enlisted. Every Friday night during the season one of the young professors came out by train to lecture to us on civics, European history, the science of agriculture, the art of bird watching, or some such subject.

Coming up by train late in the afternoon the university lad usually stayed at our house. Meetings seldom broke up until midnight, for the question-and-answer period after the lecture gave everyone a chance to talk.

One young Englishman whom we had quite frequently was a constant joy to entertain, not only for my husband and myself but also for our daughters. One night, busy with the dinner preparations, I said to four-year-old Mary, "Look dear, you go in and talk to Professor Tyrrel-Brown while I lay the table."

Mary pulled out all the stops. Newly encased in her winter long underwear, one of the most important events in her young life, Mary introduced it as a conversational gambit. Hoisting her short skirt, she said to her guest, "Have you seen my new winter underwear?" Tyrrel-Brown was suitably impressed.

The morning train left at 6 A.M., which meant we rose from our beds sharp on the stroke of five. When we got home this thoughtful young man would say, "You know Mrs. A., if you would leave my breakfast ready you wouldn't need to get up to see me off." But once breakfast was on the table (and this was after midnight), he would look at it and remark casually, "If I ate it now, I wouldn't have to bother in the morning." And that's what he did.

The civic conscience in a small community is often more acute than in a large centre, since here every family knows every other family so intimately. Hallowe'en in every village has always been a bugbear. In ours, not only did witches ride on broomsticks, but the livelier of the youngsters went about soaping windows, overturning outhouses, placing buggies on top of buildings, and generally raising hob. To counter this night of playful devastation, we formed a citizen's committee which made of Hallowe'en a night of family fun. The liveliest members of the younger set were put in charge of arranging costumes and getting our prize list, which activity kept them so busy they had little thought for anything else. It was they who persuaded everyone from grandparents to toddlers to dress, and it was they who appointed the judges. Staged in the Agricultural Hall, this Hallowe'en party started early and ended late. After the winners were paraded, lunch was served, hearty enough to fortify everyone for two hours of dancing. By midnight no one had strength enough to hoist a buggy to the top of the town hall.

The Christmas Eve carols became another village institution. Early in December every youngster who could sing, and even those who couldn't carry a tune, were organized into a Christmas Carol song-fest. On Christmas Eve this straggling group of choristers went about the village singing Christmas carols in front of the houses of older citizens, then converged on the Town Hall for the official visit of Santa Claus. Was it the joy of singing, or was it the lure of the Christmas bag of goodies, that gave such a large attendance? Into that we never inquired.

We had no reindeer, but Matthew Martin's team of grays, lavishly hung with Christmas decorations and driven by Santa Claus himself, was just as impressive. The eager children, gathered in front of the Town Hall, rushed out into the street when they heard that first jingle of bells, and helped unload the sleigh. There was enough Christmas spirit abroad to keep even the older and more sophisticated children from saying to the small fry, "That's not Santa Claus, that's just Dan Watson dressed up."

And around the year, singing became another outlet for the dozens of children who longed to open their mouths and give voice. A junior choir was organized, the youngest member of which was eight and the eldest sixteen. Choir practice was Friday night, and with forty-two children in the choir nearly every week was a birthday week. Stimulated by the sight of that cake aglow with candles, and the fragrance of hot cocoa, the youngsters sang like angels.

When this junior choir started on its career, all the youngsters wore their regular Sunday clothes. But when we began to do special services in the church and even take on outside engagements, we felt that uniform choir gowns were essential. Sitting down with paper and pencil, we decided we needed black dickies, white surplices and black tams, since mortarboards were a little too severe and too precarious for the children to wear in public. Where was the money coming from? We would give a concert. We launched into the staging of the cantata *The Fairy Shoemaker*. Stage props? The men made them. Costumes? The mothers made them. The cantata? A real success, since every choir member had at least ten relatives.

From the concert we netted enough to buy 144 yards of fine white cotton, twenty yards of black sateen, and patterns in every size. Members of the Ladies Aid came up to our house and cut, sewed, fitted and pressed. The velvet caps? Too difficult to make, so we bought them.

It was a proud day for the members of that choir and their relatives when the youngsters walked in procession to the choir loft, looking like celestial choristers.

Late in the fall, as a special treat, we took all the choir members into the city to see a picture show and have supper. This was a day long remembered by the drivers, the theatre attendants, and the snack-bar manager. As soon as we arrived at the theatre, countless soft drinks on the journey down caused the washroom facilities to be used to capacity. Waiting in the foyer for my carload of boys, I was a little startled when one of the attendants rushed out to demand sternly, "Who's in charge of these kids?" I admitted I was.

"Who taught them to put slugs in the chocolate-bar machine instead of nickels?"

What did I do? Paid up, of course—and never did find out who put the first slug in.

Since it was a matinée the theatre wasn't crowded. And since the show was *A Connecticut Yankee at King Arthur's Court*, with Will Rogers, I thought the youngsters would be sufficiently entertained to sit quiet. Not so. They jumped from seat to seat, from row to row, disturbing everyone, and again we had to read the riot act. But even this wasn't the end. Our small entourage stopped on the outskirts of town, there to get the inevitable hot dogs. Knowing the girl in charge, I stepped up and said, "There are forty-nine of us, all wanting hot dogs. If we line up the children, would you serve them as quickly as possible, and the grown-ups will pay the bill."

The line seemed endless. Finally I walked up to the counter and asked, "Aren't the children all served?"

"Served!" she exclaimed. "Some of those kids have been in the line three times."

Happily for the drivers, most of them slept the rest of the way home.

Choir practice, picture shows, picnics, corn roasts, hikes, fishing parties, skating parties—all these activities were part of the gay young life of the members of the junior choir.

Quite often I meet the former members of this choir, now grown up—each having followed his own bent. Amongst our graduates are a university professor, a clever doctor, several mothers of families, two school-teachers, a commercial artist, a minister, a dietitian, a garage owner, and half a dozen salesmen. Inevitably our conversation goes back to the days when they were very young, and every one remembers the christening episode.

Nine young members of our junior choir had never been baptized as infants, and the elders of the church thought that this omission should be rectified. After consulting the parents, some of whom were not regular church attendants, a group baptismal service was decided upon. To relieve the parents of any embarrassment, this ceremony was held preceding choir practice Friday night, with the senior members of the choir sponsoring the children. Our minister, deeply touched by the occasion, wished to make it as solemn and dignified as possible. He asked for a typed list of the children according to ages, and it was in that order that we lined them up. Unfortunately he was short-sighted, and the fifth child on the list was missed. So Donald was baptized Agnes, and Agnes was baptized James. Every member of the choir was present, quite impressed with the seriousness of the ceremony. But when this slip-up occurred suppressed chuckles rocked every row.

It was these youngsters who accepted the responsibility for the floral decoration of the church, the keeping of the music in order, the immaculate condition of their surplices. They saw to it, too, that anyone who misbehaved in church was thoroughly booted afterward.

We had so many government visitors that the house had to be kept spick and span. For our help we relied on the government employment agency in the city—and what an assortment we got! There was the elderly lady who had run away from her son and daughter-in-law. She arrived one night complete with a bird in a bird-cage, her household treasures packed in two trunks, a beaded cape, a plumed hat, and black, floor-length skirts. She belonged to the "let's-fry-it-in-plenty-of-butter" class. Regardless of whether the meal was breakfast, lunch or dinner we had fried potato cakes, fried steak, fried onions and doughnuts. Our digestive systems played out before hers, so we returned her to her family. It was weeks before the smell of fried fat got out of the house.

We had a father-and-daughter team just out from Central Europe. Father's preparation for any meal was to come in fresh from the fields, toss his hat in the corner, spit on his hands, and rub them on the seat of his pants. He would then dispose of six fried eggs. Using up the cracked eggs from the poultry pen was no problem while Sandy lived with us.

His daughter, a strikingly beautiful black-haired girl, had so many love affairs with the village boys I couldn't keep track of them. But never did we get such willing, almost slavish service from delivery boys as during this period.

This pair was followed by an English spinster who had seen service "in the best houses." Our preliminary conversation at the agency ran somewhat like this:

"Can you cook good plain food?"

"No, madam, the cook did that."

"Are you accustomed to children?"

"The nursemaid took care of the children."

"Do you know how to use an electric washing machine and mangle?"

"The laundress did all that work, madam."

Completely flabbergasted, I ventured a final question, "Nan, what can you do?"

She straightened up, her eyes sparkling. "Madam," she said with an air of pride, "I clean brasses beautifully."

We had very little brass, and during the busy season it got

mighty little cleaning, but I was desperate for help and took her home. Amazingly she was quite wonderful, and adapted herself to our way of life. When she left for a better position as parlourmaid we missed her finicky ways, her naïve impressions of this new country, and her devotion to what she considered her duty.

After Nan came Miss Henshaw. Her first name? We never did discover it. But with the advent of Miss Henshaw life in the farm-house took on quite a formal pattern. The best linen was used all the time. The little dinner bell was resurrected and coffee was served in the living-room. (Miss Henshaw always joined us for coffee).

To an outsider it must have presented a rather incongruous picture. Here was the silver service, and here was I, still clad in the khaki outfit and running shoes, my hands fruit-stained, pouring after-dinner coffee into Crown Derby cups. When Miss Henshaw finally left us, we speedily reverted to our labour-saving ways—paper napkins instead of damask, coffee from the pot instead of the silver service, and the dinner bell on the top shelf of the china cabinet. We missed her immaculate presence, but most of all we missed her light drawing-room conversation, so divorced from real life as to seem like a fairy tale.

Chapter eight

I get a government job

D OES a milch cow let down her milk more easily if Viennese waltzes are played in the milking barn? Is a high-production hen as high-strung as a race horse? How many pounds of feed does it take to produce an inch-thick, juicy beefsteak? These are the questions that have perplexed agricultural experts the world over. Agriculture, say these gentlemen, is the backbone of the country. Without proper and adequate food, industrial workers fail to turn out their quota; but when does a hen or a cow or a steer eat up more in food than is produced in revenue?

To further farm education, whether it be in the kitchen or on the land, the Department of Agriculture has organized specialized short courses in rural areas. Because of the work we had done on our own farm, and possibly because I was one of the few women doing such work, I was now employed by the Departments of Agriculture, both Provincial and Federal, to do my type of lecturing, which was most informal. It ranged all the way from high-production hens and dairy cows to canning and lunch boxes.

What did it mean to me? That for six weeks in the winter, when farm work was slack, and six weeks in the early summer before harvest I travelled the length and breadth of our country's farm districts. Itineraries were laid out by the Department, and like the postman—regardless of snow, sleet, rain, hail, washouts, or train wrecks—I was expected to stick to that schedule.

The week started at 5 A.M. Monday morning when I caught the night sleeper through to the city, and from there I covered five appointments each week. During the winter course the going was pretty heavy. Along with the men instructors I would land at the small station, and from there we would drive ten, twelve, or fifteen miles into the country. We went by sleigh, by cutter, or by snowmobile, huddled in the depths of the equipage and chilled to the bone in spite of rugs.

Overnight we stayed at farm-houses or in country hotels, where there was no heat in the bedrooms and the bedding was often inadequate. One particularly well refrigerated hotel had flannelette blankets and one quilt. I lay in bed getting colder and colder, even covered as I was with a wool dressing-gown and my top-coat. Finally at 3 A.M. I thought, "I can't stand this any longer. I'll go down to the kitchen."

When I got down I found my masculine counterpart already there, in a rocking-chair and from the knees down snug in the oven. "Move over," I said, "and let me get my feet thawed too."

So there we sat and thawed until 6 A.M., when the cook came on shift.

"Well, you poor souls," she exclaimed, "let me get you a good hot cup of coffee." Then more sharply she added, "And take your feet out of that oven. How do you think I'm going to get my baking done?"

But no matter where we went the food was always abundant and good. I wish you could see, as I did for so many years, the dining-rooms of those country hotels. The table linen was stiffly starched to keep it clean. Every table was centered with a vase of artificial flowers, around which were ranged at least six bottles of catsup, chili sauce, Worcestershire sauce, mustard pickle, and best of all, home-made pickles. The crackers and cheese were modestly hidden under a glass cover and the toothpicks were as much a part of the décor as the paper roses.

Breakfast, lunch or dinner—they didn't vary much. If you were pie-minded, you could have it three times a day, and fried potatoes came on automatically. It was only the strenuous exercise that saved us from indigestion.

But the farm meals were the height of luxury. We were always thrilled when at the conclusion of the afternoon session some farmer or his wife would say, "Come out to our place for supper." Did we ever turn down an invitation like that? Never!

Directed by our host or hostess, we would drive along the snow-banked concession road, turn in at the gate with the tall cedars, and drive up to the kitchen door. Outside dusk was falling, but inside the kitchen all was warmth and welcome. The shiny nickel kettle would be singing on top of the well-polished stove and the cat purring underneath. The oil lamps, lit, would create a pool of light which never penetrated quite to the corners. We hung up our outdoor clothes in the hall and then I was ushered into the spare bedroom on the ground floor. There was always hot soft water from the reservoir of the kitchen range with which to wash up.

We sat in the kitchen while the meal was prepared and the sons went out to the barn to do the milking. The south window with its crisp white curtains was always filled with geraniums in bloom and there was a rocking-chair handy. The lady of the house would say, "Would you like to look at the *Avondale Weekly,* or would you rather see the new almanac?" So, while the ham was sliced and the potatoes fried, I sat and rocked.

But before we ate the separating had to be done, the milk pails washed, and the boys slicked up for supper. The good food was put on the table, and the meal was always interlarded with intelligent conversation. One thing I learned was this: farm people read far more widely and assess the news more shrewdly than do their city counterparts. During supper hour we discussed the whole world.

And there was always the spice of the local news, of which we never tired. My hostess would ask in a casual tone, "Mrs. A., did you notice the girl in the red hat there in the hall this afternoon?"

Quickly her husband would snort, "Now Mary, no gossip." Then, before his wife could utter another word, he would add, "That was Bill Johnson's girl; ran off with the hired man last fall. But it seems to be working out all right."

"Ahhh, that Bill Johnson," his wife would interject, "he keeps his girls on too tight a rein."

But my host would add, "Bill Johnson's a right smart farmer."

Interesting? It surely was. All the way back to the hotel we'd speculate on Bill Johnson and his high-handed management of his daughters, and query whether or not he took back his hired man.

During this six weeks of short winter courses we travelled into well-farmed communities, poorly farmed communities, and those that were betwixt and between. Audiences varied as much as did the locality, but every day was a challenge since no two days were alike. Sometimes we had to fight to hold the attention of our audience, sometimes we were faced with experts who knew far more than we did. But I loved every minute of it and during the winter would pick up all kinds of information, as well as interesting anecdotes.

One Thursday night the three of us on our course met up with three men who were out on livestock inspection, all of us government employees. At the dinner table naturally it was shop talk, but as well we recounted and laughed over our latest experiences. But shortly we got our comeuppance.

At the table next to ours a big, red-faced man said, in a voice that carried all over the dining room, "Had a talk with Jimmie Jones today, and is he ever well set up."

"Thought he was sick," said one of his table companions.

"Well, he was," said the big boy, "had a bit of trouble with his brain. Went to the doc—Doc's pretty smart. He said, 'Look Jim, just leave your brains with me for a week and I'll clean them.' Well sir, that Jim never went back. One day Doc met him on the street and tackled him.

" 'How come, Jim, you never came back for your brains?'

" 'Ah,' answered Jim, 'I don't need them now. I got me a government job.' "

Needless to say, every diner turned to look at us. There we were—all six of us—government employees seeming to take our responsibilities too lightly. We had been publicly chastized and by a taxpayer.

On this work the constant tripping back and forth and the one-day stands couldn't help making the traveller a little absent-minded. We seldom got to bed before midnight, and to us it seemed as if all the trains left at five o'clock in the morning. It was on this job that I learned the technique of starting the day right, a practice I still follow. Waking in the morning, before both eyes are opened, I decide where I am—on a plane, on a train, on the high seas, in a hotel, or at home in bed. But before I perfected this technique, came an incident that almost wrecked my reputation. Rushing into the day coach early one winter morning, I took off my galoshes. Still half asleep, I must have thought I was going to bed, so off came my shoes. Then I proceeded to loosen my garters. It was only the startled looks of the conductor that stopped me midway. Under the cover of the morning newspaper I replaced the garters and put on my shoes. What was indicated was a cup of strong black coffee to wake me up, but there wasn't a dining car.

Since all of us had to carry our own bags, necessary clothing became almost a uniform. The men wore conventional suits, carried enough clean shirts and socks to last the week, and wore a heavy-duty top-coat. I followed the same pattern—a navy-blue suit buttoned to the neck, a string of pearls instead of a tie, and a matching top-coat and sturdy walking shoes. From the rear it was hard to distinguish male from female. There was one essential that no one omitted—a hot-water bottle for icy beds and long sleigh rides.

One of our winter courses took us to Manitoulin Island, well known to North American summer tourists. We left rail at Little Current. Then, since the connecting lake was frozen over, we went by sleigh over the ice to the island. Our driver, a really smart lad, had rigged his sleigh with a canvas top, out of which emerged only his fur-covered head and mittened hands. Inside this covered equipage was a coal-burning stove, a lantern, a table, chairs, and a dog-eared pack of cards. It was an igloo on runners. To pass the time on the two-hour journey, we played euchre with matches for stakes.

One night the hotel in which we were domiciled took fire; we all escaped into a below-zero temperature, clad lightly and inadequately. Villagers opened their homes to us. My kind hostess, whose beds were all in use, dragged in a couch from the outside verandah. Set up in the living-room, it was made up—fresh sheets, blankets and a hot-water bottle to take off the chill. About 3 A.M. I settled down to sleep. But unseen guests were with me—a family of young mice. Obviously when the cold winds blew they had taken up light housekeeping in the couch on the verandah. Stirred into activity by the moving and the hot-water bottle, they began to scamper about. When this safari took them over my feet, I rose with more haste than elegance. It was quite a busy night, with my hostess chasing the mice around the living-room while I perched on the top of the piano bench.

All the winter courses closed with a banquet, at which senior farmers and junior members of the farmers' institutes, male and female, provided the dinner and the entertainment that followed. Speakers were imported for this event, but the dinner was prepared by the girls of the class. At one particular banquet, by six o'clock the white-covered tables were loaded with platters of fried chicken, mounds of snowy mashed potatoes, turnips, home-made rolls, pickles, and every kind of pie.

The speaker that night was young, fluent but inexperienced. His half-hour address on the Aztec Indians was totally unsuited to the audience. It flowed on and on, glittering garlands of words with precisely the right inflection in the right places. Midway the spell-bound audience got a slightly glazed look but you could have heard a pin drop. When he concluded with a last burst of rhetoric, the applause was genuine and the thank-you speech quite adequate. But when the willing workers, after tidying up the hall, sat down to discuss the whole evening, the local minister put in words what we'd all been thinking. Said he, "It was a marvellous speech and well delivered. But what on earth was it all about?"

On this North American continent, organizations feel that no annual meeting, no big affair is quite complete without a speaker. Everything is provided, the excellent food, the attentive audience, but the speaker has a really tough assignment. By some sort of instinct he must establish a sympathy between his audience and himself. This is a rare gift, almost in the same class as second sight.

One day our schedule took us to a small village where we discovered every activity, including our classes, had been cancelled because of an epidemic of measles. Three women who had assisted in setting up the course said, "No classes, so what are we going to do?"

We made tea biscuts. I said to my three local helpers, "For a long time I've felt there is a different tea biscuit for every week in the year. Let's see how many we can turn out."

So in the church basement we started to work. Out from the ovens came pin-wheels, crescents, marmalade biscuits, chelsea biscuits, tomato biscuits, every kind of tea biscuit four eager cooks could devise. The products of our day's labour were left for the invalids, but from that experience came one of our more successful cook-books—52 *Kinds of Tea Biscuits*.

Did I earn an honest penny from this arduous winter work? Indeed I did. My salary was $7.00 a day and expenses, which in those days more than paid for the housekeeper at home and the farm help, and left me a little surplus to invest in incubators. But before any woman engages in work such as this she should sit down and carefully make out her own balance sheet. How much money is coming in? How much money will have to be expended for labour in her absence? Will the household expenses get out of hand? Most important of all, will her home life suffer?

In our family no member was any the worse for my six weeks away from home. My husband, being in the flour-and-feed business, was tremendously interested in the information I picked up in the course of this work. His customers were the same kind of people that I met five days in the week. Anne and Mary followed the week's travelling on their own small map and could hardly wait to get into bed with me Saturday morning to hear the week's adventures. During the week I used to pick up for them some small gift, which I would quietly place outside their bedroom door when I arrived home Friday night. Saturday morning I would hear the sound of rustling paper, the "ohs" and "ahs" of delight, and I would call out, "Come in and I'll tell you where I got it."

Although the small amount of extra money was welcome for new equipment, from this work I got something more than money—an enlarged horizon, a veritable storehouse of knowledge from those more experienced than myself. A successful farmer of sixty or over is the world's greatest optimist. Year by year he stakes his future on seed-time and harvest, floods and droughts, low prices and high prices. Here is the seasoned professional attuned to the land he works. And he's by way of being a mystic. More than once I've heard such a farmer claim that on a warm summer night, if you listen closely, you can hear the corn grow.

Then too, as I travelled the country from one end to the other, there came to me a new realization of winter beauty. As we drove into the country after a fresh snowfall, that blanket of white became almost lavender when the long shadows of the tall trees stretched across the road. Snow-capped farm houses, from whose chimneys in the clear early-morning air plumes of smoke slowly headed skywards, looked like Christmas cards. In the hilly country statuesque evergreens stood boldly outlined against the snow.

One winter the snow came early and stayed steadily until the end of March. There was no food for the winter birds and they died by hundreds; even the rabbits were hard put to survive. We had heard tales in a village of rabbits travelling miles by night to browse off the field-stored stacks of alfalfa. With our own eyes saw this sight:

It was a bright moonlit night, and when we came opposite the Anderson farm our driver said, "See, that's the way the rabbits operate," and stopped the horses. The alfalfa stack was now shaped like a toadstool with a narrow stem; it had been chewed by the rabbits round the base. There were the rabbits in the moonlight, standing on one another's shoulders to reach up for the tender stalks. The animal world, which exists without benefit of pensions, social security or soup kitchens, learns the hard lesson of survival.

The early-summer series of lectures, which were designed for members of women's institutes, started in mid-May and ended the last week in June. These organizations of rural women go by different names throughout the world, but their function is largely the same—to stimulate interest of rural women in better housing, better feeding of families, and an international outlook.

The financial arrangement with the Department was slightly different from the winter series, although the itinerary was the same—five one-day stands in every week, continuing for six weeks. Our rate of pay was the same—$7.00 a day. But our travelling expenses were paid only to the first port of call on Monday. From then until Friday we were the guests of the local organizations, who arranged our board, lodging and transport.

The routine for this six weeks was entirely different from that of the winter. Instead of living in hotels we had the rare privilege of visiting in five different homes every week. And it was one of the most beautiful seasons of the year.

The afternoon meetings were held in church basements or community halls, or occasionally outdoors, where the humming of the bees and the astonished twitter of the birds provided the background music. It was a never failing source of delight when, after the audience had finished singing the national anthem, the birds high in the trees also burst into song.

The audiences would vary anywhere from fifty to three hundred people, depending on the size of the organization and the number of guests invited. The more serious and inspirational side of the program was counter-balanced by the social and friendly aspects of the occasion. There was always a solo, quite frequently a school choir, occasionally an elocutionist. Then followed what were classed as light refreshments but were really a spread.

Social-service workers have always maintained that the reason men's rural organizations fell by the wayside while the women's groups grew larger and larger was that the women always served lunch, and had the ability to turn the barest hall into an intimate, charming room with their flowers and plants. And from my experience this would seem quite logical.

In most cases the high platform in the little hall would be a blaze of early peonies, blue and bronze iris, and feathery bridal wreath. The piano might be out of tune, but its tiny tinkle was lost in the volume of community singing.

By some psychic faculty, members of the entertainment committee knew when the speech of the day had come within fifteen minutes of its closing point. I always saved my best stories for that last fifteen minutes, to overcome the many distractions. Half a dozen women would rise in a body and tiptoe to the kitchen. Then would follow the rattle of tea-cups, the fragrance of the tea, the whispered ejaculation as to the lightness of this cake or the richness of an icing. Yes, that last fifteen minutes had to be really top notch, and should end on a high note.

Another thing I learned was this—when you're through, quit. As the late Franklin D. Roosevelt advised, "Be brief, be sincere, be seated."

The meeting over, everyone was invited to remain for tea. The tables were fragrant with freshly cut garden flowers, the silver tea services shone in the late afternoon light, and the food was perfection. The lace cloth was barely visible beneath the plates of sandwiches made from home-made bread, tiny tarts that melted in the mouth, chocolate layer cakes with frosting an inch high, and cookies rich as butter and eggs could make them. Diets went by the board.

There was always more food than could be eaten, which led to the great giveaway. Baskets were packed for the sick members unable to attend, cookies were sent home for the next day's school lunch boxes. Mrs. Smith took home half the chocolate cake baked by Mrs. MacPherson, receiving it with the charming compliment, "Won't this be a treat for our children! You make the best chocolate cake." Even the flowers were given away.

Waiting husbands, standing by with the family car, each took on his load of women as farewells were said. Back in the hall the china was packed, the silver tea-pots gathered up and the hall cleared. The annual meeting was over.

Each night for me it was a different home, different surroundings, interesting people. You can't accept hospitality, look at the pictures of the children, learn that the farm-house in which you're staying has been in that family for five generations, and not feel honoured that this home has been opened to you.

In these farm-houses the spare bedroom was always downstairs and opened off the parlour. It was in the spare bedroom that the speaker slept. One summer night I stayed with an older couple whose knowledge of local history was truly fascinating. We sat up late talking of crops and government, of gardens and cattle, of early settlers and new-fangled ways. As we said goodnight my hostess remarked, "I hope you'll sleep well, my dear. There's a new mattress on your bed and you're the first person to try it out."

The sheets smelled of lavender, the pillows were soft as ducks' down, the blankets were light and fluffy, but the new mattress was still encased in the heavy brown-paper wrapping in which it had been shipped. Every time I turned over, "crackle, crackle" went the paper.

I didn't sleep well. But in the morning the sun was shining, the birds were singing and the world looked fresh and new, even without sleep.

One day my escort from one village to the other was the rural mail carrier, who not only delivered the mail but did the shopping for the neighbours up and down the side roads.

That old boy knew every one of his families—indeed, took a personal interest in every one of them. When we got out of town he said, "Could you drive missus, while I sort the mail?" So I took the reins and the sorting and the reading began. The postcards were easy. But when he came to the letters in the envelopes, that was a bit more difficult. He would scrutinize the writing, say, "That must be from Mary Ellen. Just about time she wrote her folks too. Guess she's coming home for her holidays." Sure enough when he held the letter up to the sun he was able to decipher just enough to find out that Mary Ellen was coming home next week. As he handed over the letter to her mother, he announced without any embarassment, "Mary Ellen will be home next week."

As we drove along, dispensing round steak and baking powder, buttons and shoe-laces, I asked him, "Do you get paid for doing all this shopping?"

"Take pay from neighbours? I should say not. But they're always handing me out a fresh pie or a roasting chicken, or something like that. So it works out all right." Then he added, "I have the same deal with the storekeeper down the line. I bring him out things he needs and take back what he wants returned. See—that's why I've got this new whip."

We came to the cross-roads store. The storekeeper came out smiling. "Got my whip, Sam?" he asked.

"Sure have," said the driver. "Here it is. What's to go back?"

"Well," said this smart merchant, "it's a mite heavy. Maybe you'd better give me a hand with it."

What was loaded in the back of the democrat? A coffin. Why? I never did find out. For a mile or two the carrier was silent. Then he snorted, as much in admiration as disgust, "A whip for a coffin. They don't come much smarter than Will."

But it was up in the north country I ran into the strong belief, held by the men of the district, that women were the weaker vessels. An all-day convention at Silver Lake started at ten in the morning and ended late afternoon. None of the wives were considered by their husbands smart enough to drive the family car, so each man gathered up a bevy of women, deposited them at the hall, and then went fishing.

"When will you be back?" asked the women.

"Sharp twelve," answered the husbands, "and don't keep us waiting for dinner."

The morning session went as smooth as silk, ending at half past eleven so that dinner would be on the table sharp at noon. On the long trestle tables were pans of escalloped potatoes; platters of home-cured ham, sliced thick; pickles, hot biscuits, and pies. Quite literally the tables groaned with food; standing by were the women, ready to serve their menfolk.

By twelve o'clock the men hadn't returned; and in this district they were always served first. At 12:30, with still no men in sight, the delegates decided to go ahead with their own meal, since the afternoon session started at 1:30. We were well into dessert when the door opened and in came the fishermen, headed by the local patriarch. He took a long look at the table, surrounded by well-fed women. Then turning to the president he asked, "Who started this meal without us men?"

The flustered woman tried to explain, but he brushed her aside with, "It ain't fittin'. Now will you get our meal on the table!"

Empty plates were cleared as if by magic. Platters were re-

96

plenished and fresh pies cut. Harmony reigned and the afternoon program started on time.

Discreetly, no one made any reference to the fact that the fishermen had come back empty-handed.

In early October the annual fall conventions of the women's institutes commenced. Since each district had its own program and government speakers had to move from one to the other, we started on another six weeks of travel. At each convention we were expected to summarize our year's work and highlight the more successful doings. To climax the whole effort top-level delegates were invited to attend the final convention held in Toronto. Because of its importance the university board of governors offered their big auditorium, Convocation Hall, for the final rally. When I was asked to speak for this occasion, my mother took it quite seriously.

"You'll have to have a new suit, Kate," she said, "and I'll help you shop for it." We settled on a plain tailored navy blue, for which I had to pay the unheard-of sum of $32.50. To top off the outfit Mother made me a fine white blouse, whose collars and cuffs were edged with Irish crochet lace.

If you've ever spoken in public, you know how one face or a group of faces, because of their attentiveness, will draw your eye and instinctively you throw your best lines towards that group. When I was half-way through my speech a women sitting at the back of the hall rose quietly and moved down to the center row.

"Ah," I thought, "I'm really getting my story over."

When she moved to the front row, I was more certain than ever. So, the meeting over, as she came up to speak to me I felt as if I were greeting a friend. Reaching over she fingered the lace on my collar, then said in a tone of satisfaction, "It *is* hand-made. I couldn't tell from where I was sitting." Never underestimate the curiosity of a crochet enthusiast.

On that same memorable occasion I decided to drive in the family car instead of the little farm truck. Trained in the economy of always driving with a load, I asked Jim to fill the back of the car with our regular Friday delivery—eggs, poultry, and a few cartons of late pickles for our specialty shop. As the last carton went in the back seat, it snapped off the door handle.

"Tie it up, Jim," I said, "we haven't time to get it repaired." So in I drove with a rather untidy stretch of strong cord holding one door shut.

Deliveries came ahead of the speech; with those off my mind the car was parked at Convocation Hall. It was certainly no solid-gold Cadillac—just the family sedan, today being used as a truck.

Following the session, delegates to the convention had been invited to a formal tea at Government House. Since the attendance was so large, transportation ran out. Our supervisor walked over to me and said, "Kate, you have a car haven't you? Could you take four of the speakers to Government House with you?" I thought of the broken door handle, but what could I say? So in they climbed, using the one free door, and off we went over the ravine to the official residence. I couldn't deposit my guests outside the gate, so drove round the circular roadway to the stone steps.

The liveried footman walked down to open the car door but he hadn't a chance. "Try the other side," I said, with what dignity I could muster, "we've had an accident."

With a polite bow he reversed gears, and ushered out my guests. My friends have always claimed that I fail to take myself seriously, and they're quite right. But such an attitude has its compensations. Amazingly, that small incident made for me four of the best friends any woman ever had. We still laugh about it.

Chapter nine

The field broadens

OUR world-record hens took us into the royal circle. During the summer of 1927 Britain's two young princes, the Prince of Wales (now the Duke of Windsor) and the Duke of Kent (killed during World War II), came to Canada on one of the many goodwill missions that took them around the world.

As a government employee and a part-time newspaper correspondent, it was my privilege to be presented to both these youthful members of the British royal family and to be part of the press entourage that travelled with them. Their blonde good looks and their unfailing good humour during that hot, hot summer won all hearts.

Following the August opening of the Princes' Gate at the Canadian National Exhibition in Toronto, the whole party moved to Ottawa. There they participated in one of the Empire Trade Conferences and attended the International Poultry Congress, the first held in Canada. Since my government job meant some official entertaining in Ottawa and because twelve of our white Wyandottes were in the poultry exhibit, I was present on the day the egg was laid at the feet of royalty.

Canada's prime minister, the late Mackenzie King, was most anxious that the Prince of Wales visit this International Poultry Congress, there to meet the representatives of the forty-two countries attending. Leading lady was the world-famous white Leghorn hen from Agassiz, British Columbia, who day after day and as regular as clockwork shelled out an egg. Most high-laying hens will lay at ten o'clock today, 10:15 tomorrow, and so on until finally a day is skipped. But this smart little hen daily went into her trap nest at 10:45 A.M., laid her egg in record time, then bustled out with a high head and a proud stomach. Consequently the royal visit was laid on for 10 A.M. No stage beauty was ever more carefully groomed than was this bird of plumage. She was washed, and her feathers blued ever so lightly to bring out the color; her beak and feet were scrubbed and waxed, and her comb was lightly touched up with lipstick. At the appointed hour her proud owner stood there in his white flannels and navy blazer, his prize lightly held under his arm. Time passed. The official party was late. The hen began to get impatient. Her laying schedule was being interfered with. On the dot of 10:45 the Prince of Wales and the Prime Minister arrived. The hen was presented. But here nature took its course; with a loud cackle she escaped and laid her egg on the cement floor at the feet of His Royal Highness.

The events of this summer led to my first official overseas mission. During these two Ottawa conferences we met people from all over the world. But our closest contact was with the British delegation headed by Mr. Stanley Baldwin, later prime minister, and Mrs. Baldwin. With them was a party of Englishwomen, craftswomen of the very finest calibre. Their objective was to assemble an Empire craft show for that autumn in London. Delighted with the Eskimo and Indian work done in this country, they asked my government if I might take over such an exhibit.

For me it was a marvellous opportunity to present Canada to overseas friends. For weeks getting together the exhibit absorbed every moment. Realizing that most visitors to the exhibition had never seen Canada, we decided to use as a background a contour map of this vast Dominion. A young Canadian artist designed it, moulded it and colored it. It showed the vast expanse of our country, stretching from the Atlantic to the Pacific and from our southern border to the Arctic Ocean. Realistically the Rocky Mountains were snow-capped, while the Gatineau Hills had that purple haze so distinctively theirs. The forests, the lakes and rivers, the wheat fields and the centres of industry were all shown on that contour map. But it was too large for one container. Completed, it was sawed in sections and carefully crated.

To complete the crafts picture, not only was the Indian and Eskimo work assembled, but also the handicrafts of the pioneers of this country and the exquisite work done by new Canadians. The modern note was added with Canadian pottery, sculpture, art, and wood carving.

An exhibit such as this, organized as only the British can, was an eye-opener to me. Like every other exhibitor, my only concern was to do my country proud. As we unpacked and put together our exhibit, visitors from each part of the Commonwealth would stop, admire and ask questions. I was so busy talking that we worked all night to get everything in place before the opening. As a last touch, the long booth was dressed with scarlet and gold maple leaves, waxed for the occasion.

One day the late Queen Mary and the Princess Royal were guests. In preparation, all the overseas representatives were called into the back room and taught to curtsy properly. "Sink down, don't fall down," snapped the sergeant-at-arms. "Keep your back straight."

The curtsies were very much on our minds until the stately figure of Queen Mary swept down the aisle, followed by the Princess Royal. All nervousness vanished. Here was a personage of quality whose wide interest in every part of the world was so direct, so sincere and so forthright that all of us, Canadians, Australians, New Zealanders, South Africans and Indians, found ourselves pouring out the story of our countries.

When the Queen examined the contour map of Canada I very proudly pointed out the location of the ranch of the Prince of Wales. "This, Ma'am," I said, "is the ranch of your son." The steward fixed me with such a cold look I knew I'd done something out of place. Had I bragged too much about Canada?

When the royal party had passed on she said, "Did no one ever tell you that family relationship in the royal family is never mentioned? You should have said 'the ranch of the Prince of Wales'."

I never forgot that lesson. But equally I never forgot the light of love in the eyes of the Queen when the ranch was mentioned. The Prince of Wales was the apple of her eye.

It was during that same visit that, through the thoughtfulness of the women's institutes of Canada, I was presented to the Duke and Duchess of York, later King George VI and Queen Elizabeth.

One of the handicraft exhibits was a delphinium-blue bedspread, made in Quebec from flax that had been grown and spun on the family homestead. The dyes came from the forest, and the white candlewick pattern was so carefully done it was reversible.

Before I left home the proud makers said, "At the close of the exhibition we would like this bit of Canada presented to the Duchess of York. It's the exact colour of her eyes. See what you can do about it."

Permission was asked and granted. By this time, having been fortunate enough to work beside two Scottish cousins of the Duchess, I was invited to tea along with these relatives. It was a typical October afternoon in London, with the dusk closing in early. When we entered the modest residence of this royal couple the fire in the drawing-room was burning brightly, the curtains were drawn, and the whole atmosphere was one of quiet peace. After tea, our host, the Duke of York, said to one of the maids, "Fetch down the baby."

In a few minutes the door opened to admit the curly-haired princess whom today the world knows as Queen Elizabeth II. When the nurse dropped her hand the tiny eighteen-month-old princess started unsteadily towards her royal mother, who was sitting by the fireplace. The Duke of York reached forth a hand to help her, which childlike she brushed aside and then fell flat on her face. Beaming, the proud father said, "Stubborn, isn't she?"

The gift was then opened and admired. The Duchess, herself an expert needlewoman, said, "The stitches are so even." Thus, part of Canada moved into this royal household.

When the week-long show concluded, we packed up. But luckily I'd been given a writing assignment for a farm journal, which financed a further journey to Scotland, Ireland, Denmark, Holland, Belgium and France.

To me both Scotland and Ireland were like coming home. With a Scottish grandmother on my mother's side and Irish forebears on my father's side, I had been brought up on romantic tales of the glories of both countries. But the reality was even better than the anticipation.

One of the government officials loaned me a small car with which to tour Ireland. My father's people, whom I had never met, lived in County Donegal and it was towards their farm I headed. Not wishing to arrive at midnight, I put up at the village inn for the night. It was late October and I was chilled to the bone. The innkeeper, even at this hour, welcomed me with true Irish hospitality, carried in my bags and said, "So you're one of the Scotts from Canada. You'll be wantin' to go out to the farm in the mornin'. There's a room all ready for you."

He led me up the narrow steps to a little bedroom under the eaves. The bed was so high it needed a four-step ladder to get into it. This friendly soul trotted up the latter, turned down the covers, plunged his hand between the sheets, then said in a tone of great distress, "The sheets are damp, Missus. You'll be needin' a nightcap."

I had visions of a glass of hot toddy, and warmed with anticipation I stood there waiting. Sure enough the nightcap was forthcoming, but it was one of those knitted woollen affairs with a frill, which fits snugly over the head and tucks inside the nightgown. Still chuckling, I put on the nightcap and climbed into the feather bed. In the morning (still in the nightcap) I was served green tea, Irish scones and a duck's egg.

When I drove up the long lane of the Donegal farm that morning, I had the extraordinary feeling, "But I've seen all this before." On either side were the fields, separated by hedges instead of fences. Along the driveway the roses were still blooming; at the front door the Irish setters lay sprawled out in the sun. The farm-house was long and low and from the chimneys lazy plumes of smoke rose in the still autumn air.

"All the way from Canada!" exclaimed my relatives. "Come in and have a cup of tea." So there in front of the peat fire we had more green tea, more scones, and another duck egg.

And it was here that I first heard of cross-eyed white Wyandottes. My relatives said, "When you get to Cookstown be sure to visit Mary McMichael. She has the best white Wyandottes in this country." So off I went to the Hill Farm and this famous feminine breeder of my favourite birds.

According to our standards, her poultry-keeping was rather casual, but the proof of its success was right there. The birds, wild as hares, laid eggs and plenty of them. When I asked Mary the secret of her success in choosing high-production pullets, she said, "It's as simple as this. Before you put the pullets in the laying pens, hold them tight by the feet and look them straight in the eye. If they're cross-eyed, they lay eggs; but if the eyes meet you straight on, throw them in the pot. They're not worth feeding."

This priceless bit of wisdom I carried back home with me. Forget, I said to myself, our highly scientific selection of the birds, and for high egg production stick to cross-eyed hens.

As well as her Belfast market, Mary McMichael had her own local market, which somewhat resembled a relay race. County families wanted eggs fresh-laid for breakfast and would order a daily clutch of three or five or seven, depending on the size of the family. Standing by, and waiting for the hens to lay, was the fourteen-year-old delivery girl with her bicycle. Into the brown baskets marked for each family would go the eggs, and away the girl would whizz on her bicycle with the eggs still warm. Bills to county families were rendered only twice a year, which made me wonder how Mary financed the feeding of the birds in between this semi-annual payday.

When a Scotsman says no, that's exactly what he means. There's no if or and or maybe about it. In Scotland I ran into this unyielding resistance towards any new trends in housing, in agriculture, in religion.

On the North American continent there was much talk of low-cost multiple housing for lower-income groups. In Scotland this trend had been adopted by the more progressive members of the municipal councils. On the outskirts of Glasgow, then in the depths of the shipbuilding depression, a new housing development had been built, and was to be opened the day following my arrival. But to the Glasgow working-man this conglomerate housing enterprise was the taking over of his right to own his own small cottage, no matter how inadequate. On the evening before the grand opening, Glasgow individualists very methodically broke every window in the brave new red-brick building. But as I learned, you can count on Scottish obstinacy. The broken glass was swept up and paper pasted over the windows, and the building opened on schedule.

Kilmarnock was a Scottish name as well known to me as Edinburgh, my grandmother's birthplace. With her to Canada she had brought a Kilmarnock striped woollen bonnet—"soncy", as she called it. But as well as bonnets, Kilmarnock had an experimental farm with prize poultry that I wanted to see. It was another official occasion—Farmer's Day—when the fields of sugar beets, newly grown in Scotland as poultry and dairy feed, were to be exhibited before harvesting. Did the local men of the land take kindly to this innovation? I should say not. To them it smacked of foreign infiltration. On the eve of Farmer's Day they swarmed through the sugar-beet acreage, hacking off as many of the sugar beets as possible. But the Secretary of Agriculture was not dismayed. Smacking the lectern in front of him, he declared in firm tones, "People of Scotland, the sugar beet has arrived." Partially convinced, and with true Scottish thrift, the wreckers took home the crop and found sugar beets were indeed good feed.

But it was in St. Giles Church, Edinburgh, that the Scotland of my grandmother's tales really came alive. The Gothic crown which tops the central tower I recognized on sight from my grandmother's pictures. Just outside the church in Parliament Square was the grave of John Knox, a flat tablet set in the pavement and bearing his initials. Inside, the church was just as my grandmother had described it—the high pulpit, the beautiful choir loft, and the dim light.

At the evening service that I attended the minister spoke to the student body of Edinburgh University in a sermon lifted straight from the Old Testament. It breathed death and damnation to sinners and laggards, but promised an austere heaven to those who lived their lives according to the precepts of the Shorter Catechism and the Westminster Confession of Faith. That night in bed I laid aside my mystery story and tried to repeat by memory the 107 questions and answers of the Shorter Catechism.

We landed in Denmark along with the first mammoth shipment of bananas. This luscious yellow fruit, comparatively new to the people of Copenhagen, was being sold from fruit stalls at every corner. But in tidy Denmark not a banana peel was found on the streets. Every skin was tossed into the innumerable waste baskets which keep Copenhagen as it is—freshly washed and dried every morning.

And it was in Denmark that I learned the real meaning of farm economy. At home, hundred-acre farms, quarter-sections of land, miles of ranch country were the rule, not the exception. Headlands and fences—what did it matter! There was so much land. But in Denmark, with a farm of 30 acres being considered an extensive estate, every inch was cultivated. Here were no headlands and no fences—the fields were ploughed right to the roadway. Boundaries between neighbours were marked with stakes.

There was also rigid government supervision of agriculture. Every dairy farmer was required to grow a certain quantity of sugar beets for each milch cow in his herd. To make the land more productive it was heavily fertilized, and none of this good topsoil was wasted. When the sugar beets were harvested and taken to the municipal pulper, the topsoil washed from the sugar beets was returned to the owner.

In the dairies, instead of the milk cans being casually emptied, each one was turned upside down on an endless chain so that not one drop was wasted.

To stimulate intelligent farming, night agricultural short courses were set up in every community. These were attended by both the farmers and their wives, since this business of running a farm was a partnership. At that time in Denmark marriage meant that the assets of both parties were owned jointly by husband and wife.

Holland was reached by air, one of the most uncomfortable flights I've ever endured. The plane was light, the air pockets were treacherous, and 90 per cent of the passengers were air-sick. There was only one tiny washroom and none of those handy little containers now available on every plane for such emergencies. When we landed at Amsterdam we were untidy, unwashed and pale green. No wonder that on that day I took rather a jaundiced view of that city.

But when we got out into the country, driving along the dyke highways that keep the salt sea waters from flooding the farm lands, the picture was entirely different. The tidiness of Holland has always been emphasized. But with a backward look to my own country and a forward look to what could be learned, what impressed me was the thrift that pervaded every part of the agricultural scene.

Compost heaps were as important as the farm-house itself. Leaves were not burned, as at home; along with every bit of green vegetation remaining after the harvest, they were added to the compost heap. Dykes, constantly supervised, were not permitted to spring a leak. Small farm holdings were scrupulously cared for. Conservation of every resource in Europe was of necessity a well-established principle before we had begun to consider it.

Belgium and France were both visited on the return journey. By this time I was so anxious to get home that neither the best-looking hens nor the delights of Paris could hold me. The Atlantic crossing was rough and cold, but I didn't care; I was homeward bound.

In Toronto I stopped off briefly to turn in my copy. My editor said, "Kate, that last stuff of yours wasn't too well received. Canadian farmers don't like to be criticized." I wasn't too much upset. Quite blithely I answered, "You sent me over to report what I saw, and that's what I've done."

The drive home went like a flash. Here was the familiar

road over which I had trucked so many dozens of eggs, crates of raspberries and jars of jam, and every inch of which I knew. As I drove past the Marchand turkey farm I thought, "Wonder how the turkeys are this year." When the long, winding hill of Holland Landing came in sight I felt, "There are the hills of home. This is my country."

Henry and Anne and Mary had waited supper for me. When afterwards we sat in front of our own fireplace and my small daughter looked up and said, "Mother, I love your homely face," my cup of joy overflowed. Even the fact that in my six-week absence every pullet had developed sniffles was only a fresh incentive to doff the travelling clothes and get back into overalls.

part two••

Chapter ten

We earn an honest penny with a saucepan

WHEN, after six years in government work, I resigned, the future looked very rosy to us. The mill was doing well, our poultry business was soundly established, and the apple orchards bore better every year.

For five happy years our family of four worked together as a team, all of us busy as beavers. When we weren't canning chickens we were grading eggs. After spraying the orchard we went to choir practice. Springtime meant planting, summer brought not only canning but bowling tournaments, the fall clean-up coincided with the opening of the bridge season, and the first snow meant time to read. They were five golden years.

Then suddenly the picture changed. You've heard of the depression? We were right in the middle of it. On top of that came the theft of our poultry and the burning of the buildings, which left us all flattened in spirit and also in pocketbooks.

But there's always a break in the clouds. One day an advertising agency phoned to ask, "Kate, could you put on a series of cooking schools for us in Montreal starting with the New Year?"

I hesitated a moment, then said, "Let me think it over. Where would the cooking schools be held?"

"In large theatres."

"How many would there be?"

"Thirteen, or maybe more."

"What would you expect of me?"

"Make up a different program each day for five days, engage a staff, run the whole show. It's up to you."

"I'll phone you tomorrow," I said, "and let you know." There it was—cash in the hand—a scarce commodity in these years.

That night after talking it over we decided that it was an opportunity that shouldn't be missed. Neither my husband nor my daughters had any doubt in their minds that I could handle it; I was the one who spent the sleepless night. After all, I'd been away from work such as this for five years. But in the morning I accepted the offer and we were launched on cooking schools.

What were my assets? Being the first daughter in a family of boys, I was brought up with food, and my mother was an excellent manager. In preparing three meals a day for such a large family as did my mother, speed was of the essence. Unconsciously I picked up her efficient short cuts. She never wasted a movement. Then too, I learned from her the ability to work and talk at the same time, since round the bake-table we did homework and heard one another's lessons, without missing the rhythm of the mixing spoon.

But to move from the average kitchen to a theatre stage is quite a step. To me it meant planning a program around one product, making up a whole week's schedule so that every recipe was foolproof. It meant the assembling of a staff, and of equipment that could be easily packed; and there was only two weeks in which to do it.

In Montreal the cooking schools were held in movie theatres and were all scheduled for the morning, so that the regular picture show could open at 1 P.M. A cooking school, more than any other stage presentation, needs the intimate, homelike look that makes every woman feel at ease. These huge, bare theatre stages, exposed when the gold curtain rolled up, were anything but attractive. While the testing went forward at home, a design artist made for us a kitchen background, quite literally a dream kitchen. There were plenty of cupboards, lots of counter space, and shining copper utensils. At the last moment we added a couple of canaries that, exhilarated by the bright lights and the gay chatter of the women, burst into song.

Then too, nothing puts the average home-maker off a show as does a bevy of professional-looking people rustling about the stage in white, starched uniforms. "Dietitians," they whisper. "I'll bet they can't boil a kettle." So I wore yellow dresses with frilly white collars and cuffs, and a white apron. Our convent-trained French assistant wore the conventional delphinium-blue smock. The colour was good, the atmosphere was pleasant. We had the audience with us, since it might have been anyone's kitchen.

Because of our ten o'clock show, we were all on deck at 6 A.M. We worked to a timetable to have twelve completed dishes ready for viewing before the audience arrived. In the short period of the cooking school proper it's possible only to demonstrate the preparation of each dish, and pop it in the oven. The technique then is to display the completed dish with the comment, "Now this is what it looks like after baking."

It was strenuous work but we enjoyed it. Women react to a mouth-watering dish with all the trimmings just as men react to a new car.

At the close of each session all the food, including the containers, was given away. The lucky women took home a hot ready-made dinner, a fresh pie, home-made rolls, a batch of cookies, or a layer cake piled high with frosting. Fortunately for us, we did not have the problem of transport.

In all we covered the thirteen districts of Montreal—some English, some French—and stayed a week in each theatre. Every morning when the curtain rolled up there was the tantalizing fragrance of fresh-baked food in the theatre. We were in our fresh uniforms, the stage was dressed, and the display table in the orchestra pit was complete with lace cloth, flowers, and candles.

Every noon when the curtain rolled down we turned to the regular clean-up. Before we finished the current picture had started. We never saw it—but we heard it. By Friday we could repeat every word of the dialogue played on the sound track. Naturally there were love scenes and it was most amusing to watch our pretty little French-Canadian helper while the hero murmured to the heroine, "Darling, you don't know how much I love you." Pauline would pause entranced. At nineteen she was wide-eyed with romance.

Our work completed, we sat around on the packing boxes and ate our own lunch. We were a highly diversified group. Our dishwasher was an ex-convict who had been given his chance at rehabilitation by our warm-hearted sponsor. The master of ceremonies was an ex-Mountie who, in spite of carefully tailored clothes, still walked like a rider. The French assistant had been convent trained and our English assistant was a married home-economics graduate. Our trucker had been a rum-runner in the days of prohibition. Our dinner conversation never lacked spice.

The audiences? They varied all the way from the wealthy to the lower-income groups, from French to English, from transplanted old-country women to new immigrants. With each audience the approach had to be slightly different. For the French we used more coloured icing and much more whipped cream. With the English-speaking Montrealers the afternoon-tea-party atmosphere was introduced—pound cake and Banbury tarts. The basis of our appeal to the Scottish-born women was scones and steam puddings. For the newcomers to Canada it was coffee-cake and cardamon bread. But we all talked a common language —food. Three meals a day is international.

Some of the theatres in which we worked were old, damp and not entirely free from rats. Before getting dressed for the show I learned to hammer at the door of my dressing-room, which was buried deep on the lower level. Forewarned, the rat would move out and let me move in. Emotionally that dressing room was too small for both of us.

But then came the morning when one of the marauders, tantalized by the smell of the food, came up into the theatre itself. He scooted down the aisle; in a split second it seemed to me the whole 1,200 women stood screaming on their seats. It was left to a sturdy Scottish woman with a big umbrella to give that rat the chase of his life. Up and down she ran, shouting, "There you are! Corner him!" Finally she caught him and was given a standing ovation. This wasn't difficult since the women were already on their feet. The show proceeded but the cream puffs, usually the hit of the show, seemed an anticlimax.

That was the winter of the big freeze, such as Montreal has

not seen since. Snow fell every night and got packed higher and higher in the streets, until finally, driving from a side street on to St. Catherine Street, the car would drop 12 inches. Taxis were stalled, trucks were immobilized, street-cars clanged bells in vain. The tangle of traffic and the voices of the drivers, all shouting "Vite, vite!" became part of the 6 A.M. expedition to the theatre.

That winter I got to know and love Montreal—its colour, its gaiety, its cosmopolitan atmosphere. But people to me have always meant more than buildings. And when some guests at our morning cooking schools took to following us from one theatre to another, we looked on them as friends. Standing chatting afterwards, they would tell me about their children and ask so kindly about mine.

But the ultimate proof came during one of the shows. Every morning before we went on stage our master of ceremonies checked us—stocking seams straight, every hair in place, and make-up carefully applied. I was in the midst of making a lemon pie one morning when one of the ushers came quietly on stage to hand me a note. Opening it quickly, this is what I read: "Kate, your slip's showing." Every eye was fixed on me—was it bad news? The easiest thing to do was read the note aloud, then retire gracefully and hitch up the slip. I got a bigger hand for that performance than for the lemon pie.

Of necessity we worked Sunday morning, setting up in the new theatre for the coming week. But we timed this part of the day so that everyone got to church—the Roman Catholics to mass; the ex-convict to the Oxford Group, which had taken him under its wing; the former rum-runner to his Mission. Being a continuing Presbyterian, I betook myself to the Church of St. Andrew and St. Paul.

But Sunday afternoon was a thing apart. Friendship between people who work closely together, I've discovered, can be a deep and abiding thing. Mlle. Dubé, my French assistant, and I worked side by side six days a week. Our language was different, our backgrounds were dissimilar; so I counted it a rare privilege that every Sunday afternoon I was invited to tea at this French-Canadian home with all the traditional atmosphere of an early

Canadian family. As well as conversation, here was food that I hadn't prepared. Relaxing in front of the fire, we ate *les rillons de tour* and *pets de nonne*. And, taught by my hostess, I learned to say with the proper accent, *"Bonjour mesdames,"* and to present the chocolate cake as *gateau chocolat* for the benefit of our French cooking schools.

We finished our thirteen-week series in Montreal just before Easter. By this time our sponsor had decided that cooking schools were a highly successful medium for selling food products and asked us to go to the Maritimes, home of good cooks.

Here was an entirely different proposition. Instead of working in one city, we were to cover the main cities of three provinces. An itinerary had to be laid out, halls rented, electrical equipment arranged for locally, and publicity set up. This meant for me a quick tour to settle all these details, after which I headed back to Montreal.

There were four of us in our party, and we decided that for uncomplicated travel we should use my car. Starting out from Montreal on a jaunt that was to cover 3,600 miles, we were well spaced in front and back seats. But the trunk of the car contained in addition to our luggage, table silver, table settings, linen, and the odd saucepan that had been overlooked in the final packing. And thus laden we travelled through the length and breadth of the Maritimes.

During the next six weeks we practically lived in one another's pockets and got to know one another's little idiosyncrasies. One member of the party never spoke till after breakfast. Another would eat no dark meat when chicken was served. A third compared everything in the Maritimes with her own home town. But the acid test of such close companionship was that we all came home speaking to one another. Periodically we still get together and talk over old times.

And here is an incident over which we still chuckle. In one university town, which had the reputation for setting the best table in the Maritimes, we had two regulars every morning at the cooking school. Everyone in the audience knew them; also everyone knew they came not to learn, but to teach. The two old dears, looking like English gentry, came early, sat in the front row and commented to one another audibly as every dish was prepared.

If I used all-purpose flour, Miss Jessie would turn to Miss Charlotte and remark in a clear, carrying voice, "We always use pastry flour, don't we Charlotte?"

I would add vanilla to the creamed cake mixture with this comment, "Put it in now before the dry ingredients; you can use half as much and get the same flavor." Quick and clear would come the rebuttal: "But Jessie, we always put the vanilla in last, don't we?"

None of this was personal. Indeed the Misses Jessie and Charlotte would stay afterwards to set my youthful feet on the right path. And to show us how things should be done, all four of us were invited to high tea. The table was set up with family linen, heirloom silver and refreshments that were the epitome of gentility. It reminded me of *Cranford*.

But even that whole-hearted hospitality did not stop them from educating me in public. By this time the whole town was on to the game, and other members of our audience would say to me afterwards, "Aren't Miss Jessie and Miss Charlotte priceless?"

I too had my pride. Backstage Friday morning, I said: "I'm going to spring something on Misses Jessie and Charlotte that they've never head of."

"But what?" asked the other three members of our staff. "They know everything!"

"I don't know," I answered, "it will come to me."

Our theme that day was a children's birthday party. Instead of sandwiches, the main dish was a mound of snowy-white mashed potatoes surrounded by tiny broiled sausages mounted on toothpicks to look like ponies on parade. With the whipping of the mashed potatoes, inspiration came. Reaching for a shaker of grated nutmeg, I said, "And a little dash of nutmeg added to the potatoes gives quite a unique flavor."

I was caught with my spices down! Said Miss Jessie to Miss Charlotte, "Our mother always did that, didn't she, sister?"

There were no hard feelings on either side. Indeed both of them urged me to come back again, feeling, I'm sure, that given a little more time they could really smarten me up.

Our tour ended the last week in June. We left the Maritimes when peonies and bridal wreath, late iris and early roses were all in bloom. Homeward bound, we travelled through a sweet-scented country whose red-clay roads, white birches and green grass were in the first flush of beauty. We learned that to the Maritimers education is more important than money, that tradition is cherished and that friendship, never lightly given, is enduring.

When we arrived back in Montreal and reported to head office, I thought this work was finished; but according to the sales reports these cooking schools had really sold the product. Here was the new proposition: "Start out in the fall with another series of cooking schools," and then the rider, "How many do you think you can handle each week?"

The original thirteen weeks expanded to five years of cooking schools, done morning, afternoon and night in every conceivable spot—and every one an adventure.

During a normal year from September to June, we did 100 to 110 cooking schools in widely scattered parts of the country. Where possible we drove, which gave our timetable more flexibility.

Our local contacts were women's organizations, always eager to make money, and cooking schools invariably drew a packed house. The women sold the tickets for as much as the traffic would bear, and kept all the proceeds for their own community work. My sponsors provided the show and bore all expenses —staff, supplies, equipment, cartage, hall rental, and programs. At the conclusion of the session tea was served, for which we provided tea, cream, sugar and food. It was during this pleasant, informal tea hour that conversation flourished and for me friendships were established.

To make a smooth-running organization the whole year's schedule was set up well in advance, and from those dates we couldn't deviate, since one change would disrupt the whole program. Naturally this led to complications.

The president of one of the organizations on our schedule

died suddenly; and although the funeral was to be held the day we arrived and at the same time set for the cooking school, the latter was not cancelled, only delayed until after the funeral. Everyone arrived at the hall moist-eyed and mournful; we couldn't crack jokes or tell funny stories. The hall was so filled with gloom that finally I said to my young assistant, "Let's cut this short. What these women really need is a cup of hot tea." That day we did the serving ourselves. When, with plate in hand, I came to the vice-president, she looked up with red-rimmed eyes and said, "Too bad, Mrs. A., you didn't get to the funeral. Never have I seen a more beautiful corpse."

Weather conditions were always in our minds. We had a radio in the car and invariably listened to the newscasts, but when the weather report came on the speaker was turned up full. With rain we could cope. If there was a heavy snowfall the government snow-ploughs always helped us out. But when the sleet fell and the highways were ice-covered, we all worried. We never went through a season without the car sliding quietly off the highway into a ditch, almost turning us upside down. We never missed an appointment but we sometimes arrived a little frazzled.

The halls? The ranged all the way from theatres seating 2,500 to church halls where fifty was a crowd. One night we followed hard on the heels of a boxing bout. Everyone pitched in to get down the ropes, take away the pails and sponges, and gather up the towels. But whether the hall was large or small, there were three essentials—adequate stoves, running water, and plenty of table space backstage.

Many of the small halls weren't wired for our electric stoves, and for those we packed two oil stoves in the trunk of the car. To fit them in, the legs had to be taken off. To set them up, the legs had to be restored. Long before the "do-it-yourself" technique became so popular, we were "doing" it—and the hard way. Tools for this assembly job were carried in a small bag.

Then there was the perennial problem of the caretaker, who invariably had what is called a fifty-pound back—and our loads ran to seventy-five pounds. Only by feeding him every hour on the hour were we able to get our supplies in and set up.

Ingredients for each one of the twelve dishes to be presented had to be laid out on separate trays, so after arrival we lost no time. This required plenty of space; and long tables, we discovered, were as scarce as hen's teeth. Frequently to provide adequate space we had to take two or three backstage doors off their hinges and place them on chairs. If this reads as if we toured the country unhinging and rehinging doors, that's exactly what we did. When we started with the tool-kit, the caretaker's invariable comment was "Wrecking the joint!"

Running water? Very rarely was it piped backstage, so we had to carry a stack of pails with us. On one occasion we landed at a hall where the only source of water was the hydrant outside. Nothing daunted, two of the local women got a length of hose and really manned the pumps. Outside was the "turner-on-er", and in through the window came the hose, with which the second assistant filled the pails. The signal to stop the water supply was two short taps on the window-sill; but when the inside assistant became too absorbed in what was coming out of the oven, we had a miniature flood.

On a short run we did as much of the prep work as possible in our own test kitchen; and since the product we were selling was flour, recipes always included yeast breads, quick breads and hot breads. At home base, the yeast breads were set to rise, then were packed in a cardboard carton with two hot-water bottles to keep the yeast working. After an hour's driving we used to run the car into a side road, then get out and punch down the dough, so that it would arrive at the hall ready to knead and pan. There were always passers-by who stopped to enquire, "In trouble?" It was too difficult to explain, so I settled for one standard answer: "Thank you very much sir, but we're just kneading the bread." More confused than ever and with his head turned over his shoulder, our kind friend would drive on, leaving us still punching.

We thought nothing of leaving the city before daylight, driving 250 miles, putting on the show, and driving back home again that night. Like other constant travellers, we discovered where we could get the best meals en route to break the journey. In the north country it was the guest home run by the Misses

MacLean, whose table service looked as if lifted from the coloured pictures in the women's magazines. Course followed course—soup, the meat course, salad, and the dessert. But always at the end of the meal came the finger-bowls, with floating flowers. One stormy night when we had phoned ahead for a dinner reservation, we didn't arrive until midnight and expected only a sandwich. But there was the hot dinner, complete to the last detail. And the finger-bowls came in, afloat with pansies.

Because of weather conditions our northern engagements ran mid-May to mid-June. Since this was tourist country, we built our program around attractive and profitable food for the snack bars spaced all along the highway. We also distributed recipes for home-made jams, jellies, pickles and salad dressing which tourists could pick up and take along with them.

At this time of year many of the cottages were being opened, and amongst our audience one night was an American railway official and his wife. Both seemed tremendously interested in this canning project and waited to talk with me afterwards.

"You know, on our side of the border we have a problem which your idea might help solve," said the American visitor. "There's one stretch of poor land along the railroad right of way where the farmers and their wives are having a really tough time. A canning scheme such as this would put a little more money in their pockets, and their prosperity means our prosperity."

This was a real business man. For an hour we talked over every phase of it—how to get co-operation, what equipment would be needed, the cost, and most important of all, the market. It was then his wife came up with a bright idea. "Jim," she said, "why couldn't the dining-car service buy all this food? Just think how appealing this would be on the menus, 'Home-made strawberry jam'." We were off again. Needed would be standard small containers, attractive labels, close supervision of quality, and the support of the women.

Out of that casual conversation, I got me another job. Jim invited me to establish these canning centres; very happily I accepted, partly because of the money but more basically because it was a challenge. It was all settled that night. When our cooking schools finished in mid-June I moved over the border.

Within two weeks the three canning centres had been set up, and were full equipped. The idea, well publicized by the railroad and with the incentive of ready money, caught on like wild-fire.

Wild strawberries, wild raspberries, fresh vegetables were all gathered by wives and daughters, then brought into the local canning centre. For six weeks we made jams, jellies and pickles, and sealed them in small jars suitable for dining-car service. The women made money and the diners were delighted. From this small beginning came co-operative canning plants, still going strong and still supplying this luxury product to the dining-car service of the railroad.

Another cooking school, which started off in the usual way, led to an amusing and interesting week in Chicago. Those of us who work behind footlights are particularly sensitive to the attitude of the house. My young assistant, who set the table before I appeared, knew instinctively the mood of the audience. Coming backstage she would say, "Nice warm audience today," or on rare occasions, "A lot of battle-axes out front. Better watch your step."

This was a warm audience; I could feel the friendliness coming over the footlights. Standing at the back was a tiny, smartly dressed woman who appeared not so much interested in the food as in its presentation. When, after all the prizes had been distributed and the food wrapped, she still lingered I had a feeling that something exciting was afoot.

The tiny woman was the manager of the Chicago Women's World's Fair, held annually in the huge Furniture Mart of that city. It was a sophisticated show and Miss Bennet, who knew programming, thought that a typical farm kitchen with food demonstrations twice daily would add a folksy bit. Before she left we got down to cases. I was to provide the recipes, the demonstrations and the chit-chat; she would arrange for equipment, furnishings and set-up.

The day before the show opened I arrived at the Furniture Mart. "Where do I go?" I asked Miss Bennet.

"You're right down in the center," she answer. "I'll send one of the boys with you. I'm sure you'll like your set-up."

We walked through what seemed like miles of displays. There were imported French gowns, art treasures, exquisitely furnished rooms—everything that would appeal to luxury-loving women. Finally we arrived at what was billed "The Farm Kitchen."

One of Marshall Field's young interior decorators had set it up. To the side was a hand-carved Dutch dresser, modestly priced at $375. On the shelves was arranged a set of Limoges china. Facing the audience were a restaurant-sized electric stove and refrigerator, and ranged on the walls were dozens of kitchen gadgets. Anything more remote from a farm kitchen could scarcely be imagined. A cheap cut of meat and what to do with left-overs seemed slightly out of place in this setting.

The pot roast was displayed on a $25 platter, was served with sterling silver. The tasty left-over made its appearance in an Italian pottery casserole. But the audience found nothing incongruous in the setting and the young interior decorator beamed over it every day. After a few days, I too became accustomed to this Alice in Wonderland atmosphere and earnestly talked economy from a $5,000 farm kitchen.

Chapter eleven

Our bill of fare includes a fair

IT WAS just about this time that we started our cooking schools in Toronto at the Canadian National Exhibition, which ran the last week in August and the first week in September.

Our cooking school followed a high-style fashion show complete with lavish background, a gold staircase down which the models swept in incredibly beautiful clothes. As usual it concluded with a bridal scene. Our problem was to hold the audience while the theme swung from "O Perfect Love" to "Home on the Range". It was a question of timing. The gold stairs were moved out into the left wing, while from the right attendants wheeled in the pre-heated stoves, the refrigerators, kitchen tables, sink, and kitchen cupboards; the background with its frilly-curtained window, in which were potted geraniums; and even a canary in a cage.

In this complicated set-up we encountered two hazards—power and water. Electric cables for the stoves and refrigerators were laid along the stage floor. It took pretty fast footwork to step over them casually, with never a downward glance, and not fall flat on your face.

There was also the constant problem of running water and its disposal. It was easy enough to pipe cold water into the sink, but there was no convenient drainage. To overcome this difficulty, our head plumber laid in a dry well under the stage. When the sink was in place for the show, one of the plumbers had to make certain that the rubber tubing between sink and dry well was clear. This he did by crawling under the stage and blowing up through the tubing. Inadvertently, while he was still puffing and blowing, the assistant turned on the stage tap full force. We disregarded the strong language below stage and with outward calm went on making a party dish out of hamburger.

As usual, there were women who came every day; they always occupied the same seats and we got to know them. We looked forward to seeing those friendly faces and the spontaneous way in which they laughed at all our jokes. In the front row and third seat from the end sat a plump, jolly little woman who seemed interested in every dish we made. On the closing day when we tied up the show, she waited to speak to me, introducing herself by saying, "I'm Mrs. Glenn. My husband works over in the electrical department so I have a pass for the whole season."

"I've noticed you every day," I answered, "and was so glad to see you."

With a bonny smile, Mrs. Glenn replied, "I've really enjoyed it, Mrs. A. Mind you, I don't think I've learned an awful lot, but you sure are amusing."

On closing day we started the familiar routine of packing up, which is rather dull. Then came the bouquet. The manager of the Exhibition dropped in to say, "That was a grand show, Kate. We'd like to have you come back again next year. There's a new building going up, you know, and we've great plans afoot."

By the following year the new Electrical Building was completed. "What better way to pull in the crowd," said the manufacturers, "than with a cooking school. Here are our potential customers."

Flanked by aisles of refrigerators, stoves, washing machines, irons, radios and fans, a theatre was set up in the heart of the building. It was delightful. The white painted walls gathered warmth from the billowing dropped ceiling of daffodil-yellow cotton. Ranged in a semicircle in the auditorium were 1,200 seats. The stage was adequate and the prep kitchens *more* than adequate. Indeed we had so many stoves and refrigerators from competing firms, we could hardly find our way amongst them.

We also had an unlimited supply of utensils and a staff of twelve. That was the gayest project I've ever undertaken. Ten of the staff were young university students, both male and female. No type of work daunted them. During our prep period in the morning they swept out the theatre, dusted the chairs, decorated the stage, and sang incessantly. While we prepared lunch they peeled the vegetables, chopped the apples, beat up seven-minute icing, and licked the bowls.

At 2 P.M., half an hour before the show opened, they changed into white, seated the audience and handed out programs. Then away they went backstage to change into their costumes, since daily during the cooking-school intermission a stage and radio show was put on.

For all of them it was a new experience, another field opening up. Every one of them went on to successful careers as singers, writers, radio and TV producers, or advertising executives.

One day we did our own adaptation of a Robin Hood episode. On the stage stood a menacing group of highway robbers. In their midst was the beautiful Maid Marian, in an old-fashioned costume that swept the floor. To her rescue came Robin Hood, crying, "Unhand her, villain!" This scene we held for a few breathless seconds while suspense mounted. Even the commissionaire at the door was entranced. Ducking under his arm and walking directly in front of the stage came a mother with four small children.

"What's going on here, Momma?" asked one.

"Nothing much, dear," answered his mother. "Let's go to the midway." All action ceased as they proceeded to the exit door, waving balloons and blowing horns. Mother never realized that in the midst of this hair-raising episode the sensitive mikes had picked up her opinion of the show.

Every afternoon and evening session of the cooking school yielded its quota of amusing incidents. Naturally there were plenty of product prizes, and everything we baked was given away as well. But to really dress up the show we had three special gifts—a silver plate for the most recently married bride, an engraved silver tray for the person coming from farthest away, and a beautiful big birthday cake for the oldest person in the audience.

One afternoon when we called for the bride a rather middle-aged couple stood up. "When were you married?" I called over the loud-speaker. The bridegroom responded with, "Just this morning, Mrs. A., we're on our honeymoon." Most honey-mooners head for Niagara Falls, but obviously this bridegroom was more concerned with being well fed than with romance. As well as the silver cake plate, the bridegroom collected every recipe.

The silver trays for long-distance travellers made us delve into geography. Was South Africa farther away than New Zealand? What was the actual distance to New Delhi? The trays were really quite handsome, so visitors came regularly, hoping that one day they might carry home that momento of the Exhibition. To stop arguments in the audience we had to install a large-scale map of the world and a steel rule.

The birthday cakes? They too led to a twice-daily computa-tion. When this three-story cake on its outsized silver server was carried in, gleaming with candles, we could hear the "Ah" from the audience. One basic fact we learned—anyone over seventy doesn't hide his age, he brags about it, even adds a few years.

On one memorable day, when I called the usual question, "Anyone here 90 years old?" both a man and a woman stood up. Then started the sorting out.

"When were you born, madam?"

Right on the dot came the answer, "April 6, 1838."

From the gentleman the same answer was forthcoming—April 6, 1838.

Now we had to delve into the hour. By an extraordinary coincidence, both these marvellous people claimed they were born at exactly six o'clock in the morning. Taking a lead from Solomon, we cut the cake in half. The happy recipients went off, each with a box under the arm to celebrate the occasion with a bottle of pop.

About this time the directors of the Exhibition decided that the entire women's program could be vastly extended, create more interest and build up attendance. Since the cooking schools had drawn such enthusiastic crowds, I was asked to head up the entire Women's Division. I was even given a title—Director of Women's Activities. Up until this time my work began and ended with the successful production of the cooking schools. Now it was to cover the whole field of women's interests.

Where do you start? With adequate space. Our program included the school exhibits in one building, furnished houses in another, the theatres for fashion shows and cooking schools in a third building, teen-town—then a new and growing interest —in still another, and the handicrafts in a fifth building. Our two functions were to put this diversified program on paper, then sell participation in it so that we would break even on expenses.

Early in May, after months of preparation, we invited all the manufacturers and school executives to a supper party at the Administrative Building. This party was held on a Friday night, when the week's work was over and no one had to go back to the office. The grounds of the 350-acre Exhibition Park were at their best. Spring flowers were blooming, birds were singing, and the maple trees were in full leaf. Every guest knew that the well-planned permanent buildings looked solid and worth-while. Every manufacturer also knew that, come late August, more than a million people would enter the gates, swarm through the buildings, and be in a buying mood. These green lawns would be crowded with family groups, international buyers, young married couples, children, and tourists. And no matter how dense the crowd, the fresh breeze from the blue waters of the lake made for comfort. It was an ideal set-up. The preliminary planning done at this May meeting was the forerunner of success in late August.

At each place was a copy of the proposed program; on the walls, plans of the buildings with space tentatively allocated to the various projects. The real business of the night started after the last cup of coffee. Our guests studied every plan. Where are the entrances? What are the traffic figures through this building? Who will be my neighbour? Old established firms with a record of dignity insisted that the exhibitors in their area be of comparable stature.

When the last guest left around midnight, we started to assess the picture; for this was only the beginning. For the next three months it was argument, compromise and adjustment until the last blueprint was made.

With every day the pace quickened, and conferences were held incessantly. With us work usually ended at midnight, at which time we would hold our heads and say, "Get another blueprint showing the changes. We'll never be ready for the opening."

But, amazingly, we were. Thursday night (we opened on Friday morning at 9 A.M.) we didn't attempt to go to bed. Last-minute merchandise kept arriving, had to be unpacked and placed. Electricians, carpenters, plumbers, painters dashed about just as tired as we—and a lot more voluble.

To celebrate the opening of the new theatre the 1,200 chairs had been newly painted. When they were delivered at 11 P.M., we discovered that the paint was still tacky. We knew that every marked dress would mean a cleaner's bill, so out again went a hurried call for painters to spray on a quick-drying finish.

We fed everyone at midnight, then went around the furnished rooms with half-shut eyes, saying, "That red lamp shouldn't be next the yellow sofa." Now came the last straw. Our interior decorator decided that the furnished rooms looked too cold. "They need personality," he said. I handed him the key to our house and said, "Drive over and collect the personality." An hour later, over came my grandmother's best china, wedding presents, pictures off the walls, books, my complete collection of red glass, and even the children's toys.

Friday morning we broke off at 6 A.M. with a breakfast of bacon and eggs. But Mac, our head electrician, simply sat down and quietly wept. "I can't face breakfast," he said, "Just give me a glass of milk—well spiked!"

At 9 A.M. when the big gates opened, there we were, fresh as paint and ready to start the show. Manufacturers? Opening day was wonderful, and Saturday the crowds were so dense that everyone was happy. But on blue Monday the complaints started rolling in from the tired exhibitors: "I don't like that guy next to me," or "The lighting on my exhibit isn't good enough," and universally, "My feet are killing me!"

But our greatest emergency coincided with a late-August heat wave. The hot-water main that serviced the restaurants broke. The boiling water, instead of by-passing our radiator system, moved right in with us. There was nothing we could do about it that day. If our heat was cut off, the restaurants' hot-water supply would be cut off, and they would have to close down. Manufacturers perspired, models swooned, and the building was a mass of people moving toward cooler air. We installed floor fans and turned on all the ceiling fans, but it was still a hot-house temperature. One disgruntled manufacturer who sold kitchen gadgets, fried an egg on top of his radiator—then called me to see it. Hurriedly we orderd 500 pounds of ice cubes, madé up gallons of lemonade, and sent it round to the exhibitors on tea wagons. But the people in the aisles, thinking this was another sampling promotion also helped themselves, the kids happily shouting: "Take two Mom, it's for free!" Plumbers worked all night; by the next morning the main had been repaired and our heat was cut off. No exhibitor forgot that day; the next year, when we started selling space, everyone carefully enquired, "How's your heating system this year?"

The date of the Exhibition—the last week in August and the first week in September—always presented a problem in timing for our school exhibits. During the long summer holidays youngsters were out of school, teachers were on vacation. To overcome this difficulty, the school prize lists were printed by February and mailed to thousands of school children. There was something for everyone; classes in picture-making and peep shows, modelling and puppets, murals and dioramas, masks and paper sculpture. In the industrial arts and crafts we ranged all the way from model ships and cars to string-winders. Little girls could dress dolls or make aprons, knit or crochet, make blouses or petticoats. The results were astounding; entries came piling in so voluminously that we had to open a special warehouse. We were assured of an excellent display and the judges developed indigestion trying to add up fractional points on score cards.

To get the feeling of this vast growing country we introduced a mural competition, "This Is Where I Live". It was a class project, with a cash award of $100 to the school. But as well we offered to transport, board and lodge for three days the most gifted youngster in the winning group. The art teacher had the responsibility of selecting the young traveller. Murals done on heavy brown paper poured in by the mile. Every type of life was represented—industrial cities, farm lands, mining centers, cattle ranches, fishing coves. Eventually the judges selected the mural sent by one of the public schools in Brandon, Manitoba. The art teacher decided that twelve-year-old John Chudzik, whose parents were Polish, should be despatched to accept the award for his group.

Meeting Johnny at the airport was quite an experience. He didn't carry a brief case and he wasn't sophisticated, but on the other hand, he was completely self-possessed. This was just another experience. He looked so young we decided to keep him at home with us.

Johnny was a charming lad and we did everything in our power to show him all the sights. But home-town pride is something that cannot be discounted, especially in the young. When I drove Johnny back to the airport I asked, quite casually, "Have you really enjoyed the Big Fair?"

He answered candidly, "It's been a lot of fun. But I think the Brandon Fair is more interesting."

Every day thirty-seven fashion shows were produced to crowded houses. Towards the end of the fourteen-day period the nerves of the models frayed a little thin. Anything would upset them, even too much chatter from one another.

During the second week one of our more experienced models resigned regularly every day—but turned up for the next show as if nothing had happened. And it was this same high-strung creature who rounded on one of the younger models with the stern admonition, "Down on your knees and thank the Lord you've got a face. You sure have no brains." But no matter what happened in the dressing-room, on the runway the radiant smile never dimmed.

Modelling fur coats when the temperature in the theatre ran

well into the nineties was an endurance test. The furriers always asked that when the model reached the centre of the runway she should gracefully display the luxurious lining of the coat. But on one particularly sultry day, the girls went on strike. "No linings shown today," they said. "We're wearing only our slips."

After the last show all the girls were paid and all the manufacturers came to collect their merchandise. Then started what can only be described as the Last Haggle. It went on for hours, but every model went home with the desire of her heart, and every manufacturer with a pocketful of money. Famous last words were:

"Thank you Sammy."

To which the manufacturer would retort, "At that price it's a gift!"

The universal appeal was the children's fashion shows. Most of our little models had attended ballet classes, and so had not only childish grace but stage presence. The little monkeys knew exactly when to turn on the smile, when to look demure, and when to hog the spotlight. As long as the applause lasted they were right out there lapping it up. Backstage everyone spoiled them. I said to one of the mothers, "Now we will have Sheila next year, won't we?" She answered, "Never again. It's going to take me all winter to lick that little madam into shape again."

With three theatres doing continuous shows from 1 P.M. to 10 P.M., the fare had to be varied to suit the audience. Throughout we held to the main theme—the Capture, Care and Feeding of Husbands.

Every woman wants to wear a size fourteen dress, so daily demonstrations were staged on "Exercise and Keep Slim". This popular feature concluded with audience participation. Our smart commentator would say, "Now ladies, here is an easy exercise in which you can join without standing up. Stretch both arms up straight; breathe deeply, now lift . . . Lift . . . LIFT." Buttons popped, seams split and zippers gave way, but the audience always came back for more.

As well as a good figure, every normal woman wants a lovely

face. To make it more dramatic, our artist did enlarged sketches of the four types of face—square, narrow, heart-shaped, and round. After demonstrating the type of make-up which brought out the best points of each type of face, she would say to the audience in an intimate, warm tone of voice "Now ladies, look at your neighbour. Is she heart-shaped, round, square or narrow?"

Occasionally this brought forth candid remarks not too kindly accepted. Said one woman to her neighbour, "My dear, you've a face like a horse." That pretty well broke up the show.

Hats! Women love them, and for laughs and chuckles this was probably our best act. One clever young creature came to us with the idea that any woman can be psychoanalyzed by the hats she chooses. Hat manufacturers went for this idea in a really big way and loaned us dozens of new fall hats.

On stage we set up a hat bar. After preliminary chitchat loaded with Freudian terms, members of the audience were invited to come up, choose a hat and then be psychoanalyzed. The comments were priceless.

When a severe-looking woman chose a small sailor our expert would cluck sympathetically, "My dear, you're too repressed. You have hidden qualities of which you're unaware. Let yourself go."

Every one of the fourteen days during the fair rated a special competition, such as on spelling, trimming a hat, doing a newscast, or making furniture from orange crates. The cash prizes were high enough to attract amateurs and the spontaneous publicity sufficiently exciting to draw entrants. As an added inducement we offered every competitor a free admission ticket and a meal on the house following the show—win, lose or draw. The meal ticket and the admission to the grounds, sent well in advance, proved to be our greatest lure and our heaviest bill of expense.

Octogenarians with nothing else to do entered every competition. These blithe spirits sent in their entries for everything from hat-trimming to safe driving. With them it was just a game. Having entered the grounds without cost, they toured the buildings with never a thought of the competition but always turned up at one of our restaurants, supper ticket clutched firmly in hand.

One night the crisis arrived. I walked into one of our higher-priced restaurants, there to see a little old lady tendering a 75c supper voucher for a $3.50 dinner. The cashier, a sorely tried man, was remonstrating with her.

"Madam," he said, "you've eaten a $3.50 dinner and this voucher is only for 75c."

"But," she answered, "I always eat here on a ticket like this."

The cashier turned to me with an air of great relief. "Here's Mrs. A.," he said, "settle it with her."

We sat down quietly, this little old lady and myself. It was then I discovered that this eighty-one-year-old had entered the whole fourteen competitions, including the one for glamorous make-up, with never a thought of participating. As if it were the most logical thing in the world, she explained, "But you see, my dear, this is my summer holiday." After that incident supper tickets were issued only following the competition.

The Newcaster Competition, with its cash prize of $100, attracted not only amateurs but professionals. But excitement rose to fever pitch when the home baking was judged. Since the entries were so numerous and the judging done publicly before hundreds of spectators, a huge tent was rented for this occasion.

We tried all kinds of women judges—home economists, food directors, non-professional but expert cooks. None of them satisfied the contestants. Finally we hit on the idea of having an all-male judging staff selected by the Master Bakers. After this things went more smoothly; the contestants accepted the decision of the Master Bakers without too much argument.

But then came what we still refer to as "The Butter Tart Year". One woman, who year after year had carried off the red ribbon for her butter tarts, went down to defeat, and that at the hands of a newcomer. When the first, second and third prize ribbons were put on the tarts and she didn't even get a consolation prize, she sailed under the ropes and into the judging ring. Seizing her plate of tarts in both hands, she upended it smartly on the bald head of the chief judge. "Take that, and that," she stormed. He took it—syrup, pastry, raisins, currants and nuts. All rolled down his face and over his white smock. We had to take time out for repairs, but it surely added spice to the day.

As might be expected, the social side of the Women's Division was a pleasurable part of our work. On each of the fourteen days of the Exhibition recognition was given to individual industries, professions, or groups of people. Ordinarily 200 luncheon guests sat down to the table. But on Press, Radio and TV Day we prepared for 600. Since we did our own catering, the Press Day luncheon strained our resources. One year we decided to have lobster salad, served buffet style and with all the trimmings. Containers for this huge amount of salad—we didn't have them. Finally I ordered new galvanized garbage cans. They were sterilized, set in crushed ice and filled with the delectable salad. While I was in the dining room checking to see if we had silver, the garbage collectors came, saw the three cans sitting there, picked them up and took them away. When I came back to the kitchen the ice buckets were sitting there but the cans were gone.

"Where's the lobster salad?" I asked anxiously.

"What lobster salad?" enquired our new kitchen help.

"In the cans—standing right there."

"Was that lobster salad? The men just took them away."

Without stopping to breathe I was out in the hall, down the steps, into my car tailing the Exhibition pick-up truck. I caught up with them; and sure enough, there were the three brand-new cans, still with their lids on. The garbage men thought it quite a joke, but my heart didn't stop pounding until the lobster was again sitting in the ice buckets. Every time one of the guests said, "Isn't this lobster delicious!" I thought to myself, "Almost you had canned salmon."

Women who accompanied distinguished husbands, or were celebrities in their own right, always had luncheon with us. Amongst the many guests whom I remember were Queen Juliana of The Netherlands, the soignée Duchess of Kent, dynamic Countess Mountbatten, gentle Lady Alexander, white-haired Mrs. George Marshall of Washington, and Mrs. Eleanor Roosevelt. Mrs. Roosevelt also spoke from the bandshell to 25,000 people with her never-ceasing plea for "peace with honour and justice."

Countess Mountbatten will always be remembered by me as the quick-change artist. Using one of our dressing-rooms and without benefit of personal maid, she changed from her St. John Ambulance uniform to an afternoon-tea dress, then to a dinner gown for the civic dinner. After each change she emerged again immaculately groomed. It was from the countess Mountbatten that I learned to buy two identical pairs of shoes to rest the feet.

No Exhibition is complete without food. To cater to every taste we set up a carriage-trade restaurant, a cafeteria, and two snack bars. When it came to ordering food, we had to gamble on the weather. If the temperature soared, fruit salad had top priority and hot roast beef went begging. To wholesalers and suppliers who came calling about 10 P.M. with their order books in hand, our first question was, "What's the weather forecast for tomorrow?"

The second question was, "How is business on the grounds?" Our vegetable supplier always gauged the success of the day by the bags of potatoes ordered. It was either "Poor day, just 200 bags of potatoes," or with great glee, "Everybody out of potatoes at four o'clock this afternoon. Had to bring in an extra truck load."

It was at this time of night that our cooks responsible for home-made rolls, pies and soft desserts came on duty. The warmth of the ovens, the brilliant overhead lights, the four white uniformed cooks and the thump of dough on bake-boards is something to be remembered. Gradually the pie racks were filled and the refrigerators became crowded with Bavarian Cream, Chocolate Mint Pudding, and Lemon Snow.

For our short period, waitresses and kitchen help were easy enough to find, but a good chef was an entirely different proposition. Most of them are fully employed the year round. Our first chef, Italian-born, had been in Canada only four weeks and spoke very little English, but he was an artist with the sauces, the desserts and the main courses.

One night an important customer sent back his steak with

this curt remark to the waitress—"Take it back. It's too tough to chew." That was enough for Enrico. He had been publicly humiliated. Hastily summoned into the kitchen by the head waitress, I was told, "Enrico has locked himself in the supply pantry with four butcher knives."

"What's happened?" I asked.

"A customer sent back his steak."

I knocked at the locked door and called, "Enrico, this customer must be crazy. The steak is tender." Dead silence . . . "Enrico," I said, "Come out and try the steak for yourself." The door opened and out came Enrico. We sat down, tasted the steak, now stone cold, and chewed vigorously. It *was* tough! But Enrico was over his crisis. "That butcher," he said, "I'll kill him!"

In line with our slogan "There's no place like home", we built and furnished a Giveaway Bungalow. During the Exhibition it was viewed by thousands of home-hungry people, all of whom had deposited a lucky-number ticket. The winning number was drawn that closing night, in view of a well-filled theatre. Since every ticket included the telephone number, we knew we could contact the winner immediately. The big barrel was twirled, the president of the Exhibition drew the lucky number—50,128.

The winner was not in the audience, so our public-relations girl rushed to the phone, carried on a brief conversation, then came back with the exciting information that the man who had won the house was the father of thirteen children, was then living in a rented house, and had gone out house-hunting. This announcement was greeted by the audience with cheers. "Isn't it wonderful," they said, "that someone who really needs the house won it!"

It wasn't until Monday morning we discovered that the winner was a bachelor, rented a room in a boarding-house with thirteen fellow-roomers, and when the call came had been out apartment-hunting. The excited landlady had got things a little twisted, thus involving a comedy of errors.

By the last Saturday we all felt like veterans. Since it was pay-day, we were walking on air instead of tired feet. But there was the vital question, "How large will my cheque be?" In setting up our payroll system everyone was on an hourly rate. Since every staff member punched the time-clock, it should have been a clean-cut proposition. But when the paymaster came in after lunch with his figures, the personal element was introduced. Said our tea-maker, looking at her take: "This has got to be revised. I did the work of two women." Claimed the waitresses, "We should get a bonus. People weren't tipping this year. They were a bunch of stiffs." The potato peelers, who got no tips at all, said "Tips should be pooled." This went on all afternoon, but finally every cheque was made up and immediately cashed.

The staff party, held in the private balcony, was truly elegant. The chef and the kitchen staff had outdone themselves in providing turkey in aspic, galantine of veal, salads, ice-cream molds, and three-tiered cakes. Yellow candles and golden flowers made a fairyland of every table. It was the Cinderella story gone modern. The white smocks, the uniforms, had all been laid aside for party clothes and the guests entered into the spirit of the occasion.

Did my years of work with the Canadian National Exhibition bring me in an honest penny? To be frank, not too many. My weakness has always been that the success of the job meant far more to me than the financial returns. Money isn't everything. To be part of a project that started with a twelve-foot booth and worked up to a five-building enterprise, is to be caught up in the magic of growth, than which there is nothing more exhilarating.

I learned so much. From these years of dealing with our diversified crowds came the intuitive response to the feeling of an audience. When for every performance the theatres were filled to overflowing; when the applause was spontaneous and uninhibited, even from the stragglers, our happiness was complete.

Handling a huge staff such as ours was also an education. Unless an entire staff is enthusiastic, loyal, and willing to give that extra effort that makes for goodwill, the peak of success is never reached.

Trouble-makers have to be quickly weeded out and the intelligent workers given the recognition which to them means more than their pay cheque. The four axioms I carried in my head were: "Be generous with praise. Be stingy with criticism. Never nag. If a directive is needed, make it clear and to the point."

Working conditions for any staff must be the best. They rate good meals, clean uniforms and adequate washroom facilities. Women employees respond to ample dressing-room space, mirrors, free make-up. The men? Provide them with foot powder and plenty of ash trays.

Perhaps most essential of all, every staff member must be made to feel responsible for the successful carrying on of the job. Once that feeling is established there are no slack traces.

And here's a small point, but most important. Before every show, and particularly in our restaurants, we asked all staff members to brush their teeth and use a mouthwash. This extra concession to good taste paid high dividends.

But above all, learn to listen with sympathy and understanding. A soft answer turns away wrath.

Chapter twelve

Testing . . . one . . . two. . . three . . . four

MY BREAK into radio came about entirely by accident. We were in Charlottetown, Prince Edward Island, on one of our week-long cooking schools. The woman commentator at the local radio station met with an accident on the way to the studio and broke her leg. To fill the gap, the manager of the station rushed down to the theatre and cajoled me (in the middle of mixing a cake) to do the broadcast. To make our audience feel part of the radio show, he installed a loud-speaker; and we proceeded to finish the cake on the air. This unrehearsed broadcast caught the fancy of the listening public. For the remainder of the week the broadcast was done live from the stage of the theatre.

Back home my sponsors decided that this type of spontaneous broadcast was an excellent advertising medium; and by Monday morning, still breathless, I was launched on a new career.

In radio, contracts for beginners are for only thirteen weeks and can be cancelled on two weeks' notice. After twenty-three years of it, I still felt as did the bass player in one of the big symphony orchestras. When he retired, after thirty-five years in the same orchestra, he said to his wife, "I always knew I'd never stick with that job."

In these days of carefully prepared, carefully timed scripts, it seems incredible that I did this new broadcast with only a handful of notes. When the operator asked me "Where's the script for the control room?" I was completely flabbergasted. In the flurry of getting that first broadcast on the air, no one had mentioned that six copies of the script are necessary for the proper timing and airing of the show. To further complicate matters, the sponsors sat in the control room. During that first morning broadcast I lost five pounds.

Apparently the sponsors were pleased. From this one local station we gradually worked up to a network show with forty-four stations.

Usually a broadcaster reads only from prepared material. My sponsors permitted me to write all the broadcasts as well as doing the shows. I was allowed to follow my own format of news, household hints, fashions, and human-interest stories, linked together with music.

For years we did three daily broadcasts, five days a week, every one of which had to be different. Each one was geared to a different type of audience—the morning shows stressed the woman's angle. The night shows were for family consumption.

To integrate shows such as this meant complete harmony and sympathetic co-operation from the three of us on the show—the musician, the announcer and myself. Our musician, Horace Lapp, whose genius is so well recognized, worked with me from the first show. During the years we have had only three or four announcers, all top-notchers. Although the broadcasts were written in the office, every show was rehearsed until the completed effort not only sounded like teamwork but actually was.

So often outsiders have said to me, "Just three fifteen-minute broadcasts a day! What do you do with the rest of your time?" I've never tried to explain that the constant search for fifteen daily news items meant the quick scanning of current newspapers, not only from coast to coast but from overseas; that fashion news involved keeping in close touch with all the new trends; that food hints involved testing every broadcast item.

The human-interest stories weren't hard to come by, since somewhere, someone is always doing the unusual. No, the story wasn't the problem; it was always good. But with us was the ever-present fear that on a broadcast interview the miner, the woman carpenter, the young scientist, the bush pilot who had flown a mercy mission, all of whom had talked so freely in the office, might "freeze on mike". To prevent this catastrophe, we always saved one riotous story; told just before going on the air, it relaxed the tension.

Commercials have become such a controversial subject that this statement will probably sound incredible. *We enjoyed doing the commercials.* We never took a contract unless we were certain it was an excellent product, one with which we were proud to be associated.

Our sponsors permitted me to write the commercials, and I followed the line of the soft sell. It was always a game throwing in the commercial so that it sounded like part of the news. In radio this is called an integrated commercial. Indeed, one indignant listener called the sponsor to complain bitterly, "I'm never going to listen to that woman again. She sneaks in those commercials before I know it." The sponsor didn't fire me!

The unsung heroes of every show are the men who sit in the control booths. Voices must blend, music must fade in and out, microphones must be carefully adjusted. If the show went through technically perfect, the operator was happy. Indeed, in a rare moment of exuberance, he might possibly say, "Not bad, kids, not bad!"

Writing radio scripts, as I speedily discovered, was entirely different from writing newspaper copy. Your city editor wants the punch in the first paragraph, complete with "who, when, why, where, what."

That's not the way to write a radio script. In the first place you're not sure that your listeners have tuned in exactly on time; mentally they may not be prepared for this story of violence. The broadcast is taken in with the theme song, a warm and friendly greeting, a quick listing of the news items being used, the easy-going commercial—and you're in.

Then too, newspapers and magazines pay by the word; the sponsor pays the broadcaster to leave out unnecessary words. On a network show every "and, the, but, whereas, however" costs the sponsor $26.000, so they're deleted.

Another rule in commercial radio writing (unless it's a soap opera) is: never end on the downbeat. Tortured listeners don't make eager shoppers. They're apt to associate that distressed feeling with the product you're trying to sell. So entrances and exits to a show must always be gay, cheerful and bright. If gloom must be used, pack it in the middle.

On radio, even with a food product, long, involved recipes are poor programming. Few listeners have pencil and paper handy; every ingredient has to be mentioned twice; the program drags. We settled for quick household hints that didn't need to be written down.

To amplify this service, our sponsor periodically permitted us to mail out menus and recipes for birthday parties, Christmas dinners, anniversaries and such like. The response to the announcement of such a mailing piece was overwhelming, and for days on end the mimeo machines would clack, clack, clack.

We had four telephone lines into our office which never stopped ringing. The well-trained office staff was bombarded not only with household problems, but for advice on how to deal with straying husbands, headstrong daughters, car-crazy sons, roosting pigeons, and the neighbours' pets. But it was weddings, funerals and christenings that netted the greatest number of calls.

One particular listener called almost daily concerning the children's winter (or summer) underwear, how to tenderize a boiling hen, her trouble with her relatives, and the state of her husband's health. But when there was a wedding in the family the calls trebled. Her daughter, Christine, the flower girl, wasn't being given the proper recognition; the groom's parents omitted some of her relatives from the family dinner; were white gloves essential; shouldn't *she* stand in the receiving line?

Day after day we dealt with these problems. When the wedding was over we all breathed a sigh of relief and said, "Oh happy, happy wedding day!"

We exulted too soon! The morning after the wedding our Mrs. Smith called to say, "Christine got an ice-cream stain on her flower-girl dress. How can I take it out?"

By now we felt part of the Smith family and would have missed the daily calls.

Our broadcasts, carried over the Trans-Canada Network of the Canadian Broadcasting Corporation, came under federal jurisdiction. Policy of the C.B.C. was that newscasts, sports events and religious broadcasts were not sold to sponsors, so from those three types of programs our commercially sponsored broadcasts were barred. We could use the colour connected with the event, but never the event itself.

The C.B.C. also has rigid standards, summed up briefly by "good taste", which excluded any mention of laxatives or deodorants, or indeed any editorial comment. Very few of our carefully written scripts were questioned, but one morning I did run into an unforeseen deletion.

The situation was this. A Montreal housewife one night put rat poison in her basement. The next morning she gathered up the untouched pieces of bread and put them in her garbage can at the rear of the house. Two youngsters prowling through the lane lifted the lid of the garbage can and ate the sugar-covered squares. The effects were immediate but not disastrous. Both children were rushed to the hospital, had their stomachs pumped, and recovered.

We thought this item was well worth airing, with the warning, "If poison is used in the house, don't put it in the garbage can—flush it down the toilet."

A few minutes after the script went to the censor the phone rang. Said the official voice of C.B.C., "On page 5, paragraph 2, where you refer to the poison incident, please say 'Dispose of the poison'. On C.B.C. we do not flush toilets!"

Our morning network broadcast was heard from the fishing coves of Newfoundland to the coast of British Columbia, from the Northwest Territories to the States. To integrate this vast stretch of country, the last minute of the broadcast was given over to a mention of local events—a fashion show in Sydney on Cape Breton Island, the marriage counsel in Halifax, the art exhibit in Montreal, the pre-natal clinics in Toronto, skating classes in Winnipeg, the turkey supper at Carrot River in Saskatchewan, the daffodil tea at New Westminster in British Columbia.

We were flooded with requests for this free publicity, and had to grant them not only geographically but with a sense of proportion. From the 200 daily requests that came in we could take only eight or ten. To the others went a letter of explanation, "Lack of time prohibited the use of your notice."

Even in this neighbourly gesture we ran into trouble. "Too much social news" one group would say; "too much culture" would be another complaint; but the payoff was a long-distance call from the newly appointed president of a women's organization.

A convention was being held in her city and she wanted all possible publicity. Quite frankly she said, "You know Kate, you pay too much attention to world affairs. Now I would like you to mention on the air that we will have 600 delegates, that the meetings will be held in the local theatre, and that important issues will be discussed."

"What issues?" I asked.

"Well," she answered hesitantly, "we haven't yet decided on the issues, but *they will be important.*"

To tail off the conversation, I queried, "Now is there anything else you would like me to mention?"

"You might just slide in," she answered, "that I shall be making the address of welcome to these 600 delegates and will be wearing a grey silk evening dress with pearls."

By actual survey, what are the most popular broadcasts? The answer depends on the type of audience which the sponsor hopes to attract. Our contention has always been that intelligent buying comes from the 85 per cent of the population who are neither extremely wealthy nor on the fringe of insecurity. It is this group of listeners, with two or three children, a home, church and club associations, who spend the money. They are *not* unintelligent and don't waste time listening to a broadcast designed for morons. Busy men and women, with perhaps only minutes to read the headlines, are eager to hear the background of world events. Definitely our news broadcasts were most popular, but even these varied. The night broadcasts were both factual and colourful; the morning broadcasts always included bits of personal information that appealed to women.

Contests on the morning show always brought response, particularly if the prize was something a home-loving woman with a family needed for the house. Offers of silver, china, table linen, or cash, quite literally brought in tons of mail. Similar contests on the night broadcasts were a complete flop, so we abandoned them. Far more popular was this gimmick: after reviewing a famous world character with plenty of historical background, copies of the script would be offered. That was snapped up by teen-agers, who used this material for school essays. We did a lot of homework.

Guests on a show are always a gamble. The most satisfactory are those so filled with their subject, their interest or their worth-while endeavors that they talk as eloquently and simply as if that mike weren't in front of them. Every broadcaster has vivid recollections of interesting or harrowing guest shows. Here are some that are indelibly imprinted on my mind.

Garfield Weston, the international biscuit king, annually brought thirty British boys and girls to Canada for a two months' tour. In exchange, thirty young Canadians were sent to Britain. When I asked Mr. Weston if he would do a broadcast explaining the purpose of this exchange, he immediately agreed. The night was set, the publicity laid on, and we went over the script during an early dinner. Mr. Weston's driver, caught in heavy traffic, failed to reach the restaurant on time. The transport of our distinguished guest and the two British boys was left to me.

As usual my car, doubling as a truck, was filled to the roof with office supplies, sacks of mail, and groceries. Perched on top of a dozen rolls of toilet tissue, Garfield Weston's only comment was, "Softest ride I've ever had!"

Karl Freifeldt also did a memorable broadcast. Before Education Week, a member of the Board of Education asked that this sixteen-year-old Czech boy, who had made phenomenal progress in his high school, be taken on the air. To further highlight the interview all members of the board and Karl's schoolmates had been asked to tune in. The rehearsal went perfectly. But on the air I tossed him an unexpected question. "Karl, how would you compare your native city, Prague, with Toronto?"

Said Karl, "I love Toronto, but it's a damned ugly city."

Quickly I interjected, "On Canadian radio we aren't allowed to use words like that."

Just as quickly, he came back with "But it *is* a damned ugly city." Listeners chuckled, but members of the board were a little perturbed.

When Queen Elizabeth, now the Queen Mother, made her appearance at a Washington garden party, her make-up was done by an Elizabeth Arden cosmetician whom she had brought from London. It was a hot day even for Washington, and guests remarked on how marvellously cool the Queen looked. We thought the secret of her make-up would make a good broadcast, and invited her cosmetician to come on the air with us.

Miss Whitney had never done a broadcast, so to make things a little easier, we gave her a list of questions. She looked them over, then made a few notes on sheets of yellow paper. During rehearsal we explained, "When the green light goes on over the clock we're on the air." We got our signal but Miss Whitney was too absorbed to notice it. During the theme song, the commercial and the introduction of our guest, those yellow papers rattled incessantly. A little unnerved, I went into the first question.

"Miss Whitney, you did the Queen's make-up in Washington, did you not?"

Quite unconcerned and powdering her nose, she said, "Yes indeed. Is my nose shiny? And it was such a hot day."

A little rocked, I went on, "The Queen looked cool and charming all through the afternoon. What was the secret of the make-up?"

Answered Miss Whitney, "Good gracious, I've dropped that sheet under the piano. Just a minute until I find it."

Music fill . . . while Miss Whitney delved under the piano. We went back at it again.

"Miss Whitney, what was the secret of the Queen's make-up?"

"Well," said Miss Whitney, "the Queen has a beautiful skin . . . do you think I should go into that? It was so hot that I was really worried. But the Queen kept saying to me, 'Don't worry Molly, just take your time'."

We took all the time there was—hunting for those yellow

sheets. In the meantime Molly kept throwing in all kinds of extraneous remarks, such as, "You know those Washington women use far too much rouge . . . Have you tried our new lipstick? It's wonderful. It would do more for you than the shade you're wearing."

Finally that terrible twelve minutes was over and we signed off. It was at this point that our Miss Whitney looked up innocently to say, "When do we go on the air? I'd better get these notes sorted out."

Horace summed it up quite neatly by saying, "It's all over Miss Whitney, just relax."

Was Miss Whitney perturbed? Not a bit. Walking out of the studio, she confided to us, "You know, broadcasting isn't as nerve-racking as people make out. I quite enjoyed it."

Sponsors, as everyone knows, are pretty important people, and when they make an appearance the applause of the audience means a great deal to them. The senior member of our firm was a courtly, dignified old gentleman who honoured us with his appearance about once a year. One anniversary when we had a theatre audience, and Mr. Benson was expected, I said to the audience, "Now when Mr. Benson comes on the stage, don't sit on your hands. He pays for this show."

Midway in the program a white-haired gentleman walked on stage; the audience really clapped, spontaneous applause such as any sponsor would enjoy. Unfortunately it was premature. Instead of our sponsor, it was the head technician testing one of the mikes. He was quite overcome, and so was I. But this outburst was just a warm-up. When Mr. Benson finally appeared, the clapping raised the roof.

Radio audiences, we discovered, are not terribly impressed by big names. A celebrity is only as good as the story told. What listeners want is that the interview be fast-paced, sparkling, and full of human interest.

The guest list provided a mixed grill. Following delegates to the Boy Scouts' World Jamboree came an interview with famous couturier Christian Dior. The Cranberry Queen of

North America preceded Count Sigvard Bernadotte of Sweden. Returned missionaries brought as many phone calls as did Guillaume of Paris. The Rockettes from Radio City Music Hall somewhat upset the technicians, for one of them, showing us how they did their high kicks, knocked over her microphone. After Dame Flora MacLeod our phones resounded with Scottish brrrr's.

Famous politicians such as the Honourable Lester B. Pearson and Prime Minister John Diefenbaker were mike-trained and politically expert. Their interviews were smooth and non-partisan.

But it was always the children on the show who stole the hearts of the audience. One Christmas Eve we did a broadcast with bed patients at the Sick Children's Hospital. On crutches they hopped to the mike or we carried the equipment to the bed. The clear childish voices, the disregard of infirmity or illness, left all of us with a catch in the throat.

Remote broadcasts were done from every conceivable spot and under every conceivable set of circumstances. Organizations, desirous of publicity or additional funds with which to carry on their community enterprises, would request a live broadcast. Our sponsors, public-relations-minded, would pass on these requests to us with their own recommendations.

Consequently we did remote broadcasts everywhere—on the waterfront following the big swim, in theatres, at annual dinners, in supermarkets, at airports, or at apple festivals. We broadcast fashion shows and fall fairs, the opening of Parliament, and church anniversaries.

This meant transporting not only equipment and technicians, but also the three members of our group. If the location was within driving distance I drove, while the boys concentrated on the script. One of these remotes originated in a Hamilton church. The traffic was heavy, the directions to the church not too clear. This, along with the one-way streets which confused us still more, delayed our arrival. Just five minutes before the show went on, we entered the church in a rather breathless condition.

The program convenor, a meticulous soul, was pacing up and

down. She knew we would never get the show on in time. We did! Everything went smoothly; the show aired well and the audience seemed delighted.

When it was all over we retired to the vestry, there to draw the first deep breath in two hours. We thought possibly we might get the conventional pat on the back. But instead came a straight-from-the-shoulder comment. Said the convenor of the occasion, "For such a disorganized group of people, I think you did not badly. Are all your broadcasts like this?" Thoroughly chastened, we drove home.

Three daily broadcasts, thirty-nine weeks of the year, can't be dreamed up by sitting behind a desk. Both our sponsors and the listening public expected me to cover not only local news but national and international stories. Exciting events, trouble spots, colourful ceremonies were all part of the broadcast material.

To facilitate this schedule we used, as well as our local stations, the network facilities of the Canadian Broadcasting Corporation, N.B.C. and C.B.S. in New York, and B.B.C. in London, England. This gave us a three-fold coverage—local, national and international.

But no matter where we were, the daily broadcasts had to come through as regular as clockwork. Arrangements for remote broadcasts had to be set up well in advance so that studios, operators and cleared lines were available. But with modern air transport we could fly the ocean overnight, and broadcast the show next morning from London, England.

Inevitably broadcasts sort themselves out as dramatic, romantic, colourful, exciting, fantastic, or downright amusing. This was dramatic:

One August night, just after midnight, an unsponsored sixteen-year-old, Marilyn Bell, started to swim across Lake Ontario, hitherto unconquered. No one expected her to be successful; but as hour after hour she fought her way through those icy waters, excitement mounted. Towards sundown thousands of people gathered along the lake front, stirred by this youthful, magnificent endeavour. My sponsors caught me at the studio, said, "We arranged for a telephone to be put in your car. Get down to the waterfront. The minute that girl lands, phone through the story." That was one of the most difficult broadcasts I ever did. Every broadcaster felt that mere words were inadequate in describing this feat. Emotionally exhausted but thrilled beyond belief, we told our story.

Chapter thirteen

Elizabeth, Princess and Queen

THE wedding of Princess Elizabeth and her subsequent
coronation as queen were two different stories—one was
romance, the other the dedication of a young sovereign.
I planned my flight so that I should arrive in London two
days before the wedding—two exciting days. After years of
austerity, the grey old city was in the throes of a romantic re-
juvenation. New material was still rationed, but from somewhere every householder unearthed old bunting, stored flags,
and decorations. All were carefully pressed and hung with
exactitude. Thus did the city show its concern that everything
possible should be done for the marriage of a beloved daughter.

This was a love marriage that touched the hearts of everyone. Over the week-end London was crowded to the last room-
ing-house. All day Monday every bus, every train, every tram
brought in additional crowds. The proud young guardsmen at
Buckingham Palace had thousands of admirers. Even the
painters, doing the last-minute touch-up on the stands, were
treated as if they were part of the royal procession.

Following the rehearsal in Westminster Abbey, all traffic was
halted as the royal party emerged. Queen Elizabeth was in rose,
Princess Margaret in beige, and the bride-to-be Elizabeth, in the
misty blue so becoming to her. The King and the bridegroom
were in full naval uniforms. On that dull November afternoon,
with the light streaming from the Abbey, the picture was perfect.
The feeling of family unity swept over the crowd like a bene-
diction; even the cheers were muted.

Monday night the streets of London were like a carnival.
Crowds milled everywhere, flowing over from the sidewalks to

the roadway. Show people put on their acts, all of which were greeted with light-hearted laughter. Everyone knew that the stag party for Philip was being held in the Dorchester Hotel. By ten o'clock, when the dinner broke up, it was hard to find standing room in that tiny sweep of driveway fronting the hotel. The uniformed doormen, the golden chrysanthemums massed in the flower boxes decorating the front façade of the hotel, the floodlights, the excited spectators—all made a perfect exit for the dinner party.

Then occurred one of the warm and personal touches that are a broadcaster's dream. I was standing at the private entrance from which the party emerged, chatting with Canadian Prime Minister Mackenzie King. The doorman, swinging open the door for Philip, said, "Good luck tomorrow, sir." Philip shook hands with him and went on his way. Gazing after the party, the doorman said, "Lucky stiff!"

That night the space in front of Buckingham Palace was a solid mass of faces. The crowd was so tightly pressed together you couldn't see the bodies. Even the dignified statue of Queen Victoria, facing the palace, had its garland of adventurous youngsters whom the police couldn't dislodge.

When the royal family appeared on the balcony, cheers swelled in a crescendo and comments were freely tossed about. Said one woman to her friend, "The King looks tired." Her neighbour retorted, "It grieves him to lose his daughter. My Bill felt the same way when Gladys was married."

The final appearance, towards midnight, was the young Princess with Philip, Duke of Edinburgh. Odd, isn't it, how tiny details are etched in one's memory? Looking back on that scene, I remember the soft woodland green of the dress worn by the Princess, the gleam of the engagement ring on her finger, and the gentle way she laid her arm over that of Philip. Obviously here were two young people very much in love.

No one went to bed that night. Sightseers filled every available inch of space along the processional route. They spent the night cat-napping, drinking hot cocoa, eating sandwiches and talking. The older people harked back to previous royal weddings and coronations. Indeed some of them remembered the old Queen's Diamond Jubilee, with its world-wide pageantry.

The ceremony in the Abbey was touching and beautiful, but even with a royal wedding the unpredictable happens. Prime Ministers of the British Commonwealth were seated in the tiers of choir seats facing the altar. When Mr. Churchill, then Leader of the Opposition, entered the Abbey he was greeted with applause. Flushed and smiling, he proceeded to the section occupied by the Commonwealth prime ministers. They too applauded him. Instinctively as he reached the end of the aisle he turned to the right, and almost sat on the knee of the Prime Minister, Clement Atlee. Every elder statesman burst into laughter. Was Mr. Churchill perturbed? He was amused; with a bow to Mr. Atlee, he turned to the left and took his place.

Following the ceremony, every overseas broadcaster sped to the appointed studio. The time for our overseas beams had been laid on months in advance, and since the B.B.C. facilities were crowded to their capacity, we each had a deadline. My broadcasts were done from B.B.C. headquarters in Oxford Street, three floors below street level.

Rather than wait for the elevator, I took the steps three at a time and arrived at C-47 breathless. But B.B.C. has a way of coping with that difficulty. While I sorted my notes and tried to catch my breath a cup of strong tea, heavily sugared, appeared at my elbow. Within the half-hour allotted to me I did six five-minute segments, then went back again to join the crowds celebrating in the streets.

Canadian, British and American broadcasters will never forget the Royal Tour of 1951! Members of the British royal house, whose Commonwealth countries circle the globe, are expected to pay these state visits, thus serving to unite the family. Canada and the United States had never had so young a royal couple, or one on whom responsibilities rested so heavily. The twenty-five-year-old Princess had left at home her ailing royal father and her two small children. Towards the end of this lengthy tour we sometimes thought that the slender young shoulders of the Princess bore too heavy a burden.

To those of us who covered the royal tour, a day-by-day itinerary was essential. But I discovered something more was necessary. Since usually I rushed from a royal function to the nearest broadcast station, I carried along with me a list of suitable adjectives culled from Roget's Thesaurus. What adjectives are suitable in describing a princess? Sorted for suitability, they run like this: charming, youthful, radiant, slender, gentle, lovely, petite, gracious, smiling or serious. As for Philip, it had to be: handsome, gregarious, democratic, easy, casual, intent, amused, deferential.

The ceremonies? They too had their prescribed adjectives: colourful, history-making, delightful, informal—and when I lacked a phrase—imbued with the spirit of the occasion. No matter how you shuffle these adjectives, some of them must be repeated. The problem was not to repeat them in the same sentence.

The press car attached to the royal train always provided amusing atmosphere. Newspaper correspondents were not too entranced with radio broadcasters. Broadcasters felt they had the edge on newspaper people, since their reports went on the air immediately.

Then too, the British segment felt this was their show. Didn't the Princess live in London? Canadians were equally certain that the show belonged to them. They were the hosts of the occasion. The Americans constantly had the attitude "Go on, show us! Can you put on anything comparable with an inauguration?"

It wasn't necessary to hear these people talk to identify them. The British press travelled in baggy tweeds, the Americans rejoiced in sports jackets, and the Canadians wore the conventional grey flannel suit.

Turning out a different story every day was nerve-racking, since, except for geography, occasions varied only slightly. There was always the guard of honour, the red carpet, and the presentation to the Princess of the bouquet. This honour always fell to the daughter of a prominent civic official. But the smartest feminine writer undoubtedly was with the American press. Quietly situated in her hotel room with a rented radio, she listened to all the broadcasts, then wrote her story. And it was good. Not buffeted by crowds, never standing for hours, never cold or tired, she turned in the most amazing eyewitness accounts I have ever read. Indeed, they were so good that on her return her newspaper awarded her a medal of merit and raised her pay.

During all these hectic weeks when broadcasts had to be done daily, what stands out?

The arrival at twilight of the royal couple in Toronto. Because of the dense crowds lining the traffic lanes from the airport, it was half an hour behind schedule. The official reception was held at the city hall in downtown Toronto. Huge red banners swathed the historic old building from top to bottom. Above, floodlit flags moved quietly in the still autumn air. The red carpet, another splotch of crimson, covered the steps. The waiting crowd was restless and the air was chilly. Just as the lights of the entourage blinked up from the lake shore and everyone stood at attention, a grey alley cat from the restaurant just across the city square decided to join the party. Insinuating her way through the legs of the crowd she walked up the red carpeted steps to the dais, turned around, faced the crowd and leisurely washed her face. Her whole attitude seemed to say, "Can't a cat look at a queen?" As two dignified city-hall guards rushed out to chase pussy off the red carpet, the tension broke, the crowd roared with laughter, and Princess Elizabeth and her husband walked up the steps on a wave of warm humanity.

Public officials across Canada, whose privilege it was to welcome the royal party, took themselves very seriously. On one memorable day, the young Princess opened a new civic hospital. Accompanied by the Mayor, Her Royal Highness walked down the red carpet. His Worship became so excited that gradually he edged her off the magic strip. The movie cameras caught that for posterity. Here was Her Royal Highness walking on the grass, while His Worship had the red carpet all to himself. I wonder what he thought when he saw that movie at the local theatre?

The early morning church service at Niagara-on-the-Lake was one of the simplest and one of the most memorable occasions of the tour. Here we had a historic old church, the thin sunshine of an autumn morning, the last of the yellow leaves, and the ringing of bells. The still green lawns surrounding the church were packed with Sunday-school students, Girl Guides, senior citizens and their families. This was no social event, but rather a young husband and wife walking quietly into a church whose service they knew. That morning the Princess wore a red suit, the colour of a robin's breast in springtime. It was banded in black velvet which matched the small hat.

The church, one of the oldest in Canada, was modestly decked with white chrysanthemums. The service, which varied not a whit from the regular service, was conducted by the rector himself. With the prayer for the King's Majesty "Most heartily we beseech, with Thy favour to behold our most gracious sovereign Lord, King George," every heart went out to the young Princess. For her this was a personal prayer for her beloved father, ill at home.

On the visit to Washington, the Americans really came into their own. There was an easy informality that we all enjoyed. The tone was set by President Truman, meeting the royal couple at the airport. He grasped the hand of the Princess and said, "My dear, I'm so glad to see you."

The press interview was exactly like the *première* of a new Hollywood picture. The red-coated Mounties stood impassive and expressionless as flash bulbs exploded, movie cameras moved in and photographers shouted, "Look this way, Liz," or "Philip, give with the smile."

But the reception at the British Embassy was the perfect climax to the visit. Since the Embassy couldn't hope to hold the 2,200 invited guests, a huge marquee was set up in the garden, and to warm it a complete circle of small electric heaters ringed the inside wall. The buffet table groaned with food. There were hot bites, cold sliced turkey and ham, salads, frozen desserts. And since refreshments included buttered crumpets, Dundee pound cake and tea, the British contingent was completely happy.

For most of us it was a farewell party since almost directly afterward the royal couple flew home.

Amongst our other royal assignments for broadcasting were the coronation of Queen Elizabeth, the dedication of the Commonwealth Air Memorial at Runnymede, and the Victoria Cross Centenary, all in Britain. Each one required the same careful preparation, the early request for air flights, the setting up of transatlantic beams and studio facilities.

The coronation necessitated the most intensive advance planning. Hotel accommodation had to be laid on, passes arranged for, and transport assured. Most imoprtant of all, the details of the five-hour ceremonial had to be so familiar that the broadcast would flow without any slip-ups.

On the overnight transatlantic flight, I reviewed the order of service, inch by inch. Since this was an occasion which would not be repeated and since these broadcasts were tremendously important, I didn't sleep as well as usual. But when we arrived at London airport the feeling of excitement was contagious.

Planes were landing from all parts of the world. As each foreign delegation arrived, the flag of its country was run up the flagpoles along the airstrip. Here were colour, pageantry and a babble of foreign voices. "Look," someone would say, "there's the party from India," or "The Australians have landed," or "Here come the representatives from the Gold Coast."

As we drove up to the city every row of flats, every tiny shop, every restaurant, every industrial plant was flag-bedecked. Barely taking time to check into my hotel, I went sight-seeing. Almost overnight, London had become a floral city. The streets leading to the palace were overhung with great golden baskets in which bloomed every English flower. Bond Street, Piccadilly, Regent Street, Birdcage Walk, all had conforming decorations, a symphony of colour. More touching still were the tiny window-boxes, beloved of Londoners, installed on every ledge and blooming bravely.

Everywhere in London was the sound of hammering and the smell of fresh paint. Stands along the route were being finished by the carpenters; as the last nail was driven, the painters moved in. Uneasy shop-owners were fitting wooden barricades in front of plate-glass windows and road barriers were being set up. As if by magic, arrows designating the line of the processional were being erected, and the colour-film merchants were doing a land-office business.

My sponsors had asked me to fly over three days in advance of the coronation, so that I could not only beam back broadcasts but also take pictures of the pre-coronation activities. Saturday, Sunday and Monday I toured the city in a cab, shooting pictures from the tops of monuments, inside restaurants, and from the back seat of the taxi. To expedite the arrival of the film in Canada, a courier called at the hotel every afternoon at five o'clock to pick up the day's take and deliver it to the airport.

This lad, a former member of the London Metropolitan Police, could get through traffic like an eel; he seemed the logical answer to the problem of transport on the day of the coronation. Not only did I have to get to the Abbey in time for the ceremony, but had to take advance pictures of the crowds, the arrival of celebrities, and portions of the procession. With the consent of Scotland Yard, my official car pass was placed on the courier's motorcycle; and a side-car was added which would accommodate not only the camera and myself but also my coronation outfit, carefully packed in a box.

Our Canadian pre-coronation dinner ended at 2 A.M. Three hours later, at five o'clock, the courier and I were on our way. We went first to Kensington where the military bands were quartered, then broke for breakfast. Trafalagar Square, a strategic point of the procession, was our next objective and a very happy one. British crowds, always co-operative, offered us every assistance. Seeing the poised camera, two sturdy workmen said, "We'll hoist you up miss and you'll get a real good view."

By mid-morning a misty drizzle had turned into a downpour. Although it did not dampen the spirits of spectators, it did cut off the view. Lords and ladies *en route* to the Abbey hastily had the chauffeur run up the car top. But six-foot-three Queen Salote of Tonga was impervious to the weather (it always rains in Tonga). In her full regalia of red robes and a feathered headdress she beamed, waved and mopped rain from her face. Cheers followed every foot of her progress to the Abbey.

By this time both the courier and myself were soaked to the

skin, but we had our pictures. Before leaving for the airport with the film, he delivered me to one of the rear entrances of the Abbey. Luck was with me; a word from him and I was allowed to change into my coronation outfit in a small back room. Through the kindness of friends my seat was in the section set aside for Lesser Nobility.

The coronation ceremony is as old as England and as impressive as history. But the memory that remained with me was the look of dedication on the face of the young monarch. I had seen her in every phase of her life—as a child just learning to walk, as a young A.T.S. recruit, as a radiant bride, as a charming ambassador for her country. But on this coronation day the soft, youthful roundness of the face was gone; character had emerged. From where I sat and as the ceremony proceeded, noticeable was the gradual paling of the face and the tiny lines of strain. The heavy gold vestments of office, the crown, the responsibilities of state seemed a heavy burden for a young queen. But leaving the Abbey we were all convinced that here was a regal strength.

At six o'clock that night I left London Airport for Dorval, Montreal. Here was another long transatlantic flight filled with the sorting over of phrases, eliminating adjectives, trying to bring a living, breathing picture to our air audience. There was no time to write a proper script so I had to rely on over-all impressions of the immense dignity of the coronation and the vivid impact of its pageantry and solemnity.

And here is a confession of weakness. I was childishly pleased that the first eyewitness account to be broadcast on Canadian soil emanated from our studio.

The Battle of Britain, fought in the sky, was a joint effort of every member of the British Commonwealth of Nations. Winston Churchill expressed the admiration of the British people for this heroic battle with the memorable phrase: "Never in the field of human conflict was so much owed by so many to so few."

To commemorate the heroic sacrifice of these young lives, an Air Force Memorial was built at Runnymede, home of the Magna Carta. This beautiful monument, austere and dignified, was officially dedicated one October day, eight years after World

War II had ended. To this ceremony were invited the families of the missing airmen whose bodies had never been recovered or given an official grave. This was their cemetery, this their tomb, this their monument.

Because so many of our listeners had sons and husbands thus remembered, because so few of them could attend this memorial service, I went to Runnymede. Walking through the massive bronze doors, we entered a walled quadrangle surrounding a green lawn, open to the skies in which the young airmen had flown. Marble plaques lined the cloistered walls of the quadrangle. These, dedicated to each country of the Commonwealth, carried the names of the missing airmen.

On this day it was a singularly quiet crowd. Here were sorrow and heartbreak, but here also was a feeling of fulfilment. For these lost young airmen, no grave could be tended since no mother there present knew where her son was buried, or indeed if he had been buried. But the permanent record was carved in marble for all to see . . . "Missing, Reported Lost, September 28th, 1940, Flight Lieutenant James Andrews."

Queen Elizabeth dedicated this memorial in a short and simple ceremony which touched all hearts. Placing the first wreath against the bronze door, she was followed by the prime ministers of the Commonwealth. Each carried the tribute of his country to its gallant sons. Then the memorial was officially declared open.

Relatives from every country walked quietly around the cloister, laying their own personal tributes at the foot of the plaques. Some were conventional wreaths; others were a sheaf of chrysanthemums or a spray of late-blooming roses.

My concern was not only to do a broadcast but also to take back pictures of the Canadian plaques showing every name. This meant waiting until the crowd had thinned. But by singular good luck we got our picture while the Queen Mother was talking to a small nine-year-old Canadian boy who had placed his tribute to the father whom he had never seen.

Since the ceremony was on Saturday and I was lucky enough to catch my plane back to Canada, reproductions of the pictures were despatched to Canadian mothers by Monday afternoon.

The Victoria Cross Centenary held in London, June 1956, came in our last broadcasting week before breaking for the summer. Since this is the slow season in radio, common sense told me I shouldn't go. But my heart overruled my head. On this occasion would be gathered the world's greatest aggregation of heroes, regardless of rank, colour or wealth. So I flew to London.

When Queen Victoria originated the Victoria Cross for Valour in 1856, she little dreamed that her great-granddaughter, one hundred years later, would call to London all living holders of the Victoria Cross. During this hundred years the tiny, inconspicuous medal had been awarded to only 1,347 men, two-thirds of whom were now dead. It was an occasion which I felt would occur only once in a lifetime. I wanted to see it, sense it, feel it and remember it.

The Centenary included three important events—the service in Westminster Abbey, the royal garden party, and the review of the Victoria Cross holders in Hyde Park.

The service was dedicated to the V.C. holders, who occupied the seats of honour. Members of the royal family absented themselves from this ceremony so that all glory should be given the heroes of the occasion. As they marched in, some young, some middle-aged and some old, the red-surpliced boys' choir sang in high, light and clear voices an old Bunyan hymn.

Following the prayers came the sermon. The oldest V.C., his coat covered with medals, was little and frail. Throughout the sermon he slept quietly, his transparent hands folded in his lap. But when the choir broke into "Fight the Good Fight", he stood straight as a ramrod and sang every verse.

The royal garden party was a gay, happy occasion. Here was no stiffness or formality, but the meeting together of old friends. To me, one of the most significant features was this: no V.C. holder, questioned as to how he got his medal, would recount the story of his heroism. It was always, "Oh, it wasn't much, you should have seen the boys that were with me." Modesty as well as valour would seem to be an attribute of these men.

Tuesday, June 26th, the day of the review in Hyde Park, brought what Londoners call "queen's weather". The sky was clear and unclouded, the sun brilliant, and the air fragrant with flowers and fresh-cut grass. The 300 V.C. holders arrived early and were played in with military bands. Some twenty-three of them were in wheelchairs, but they too had their guard of honour. Then circling the green oval came the royal carriage.

Standing in the same spot where Queen Victoria had stood a hundred years before, the young Queen welcomed her be-medalled guests. Walking through their ranks, she reviewed them. For the young there was a nod and a smile; for the old there was the warm hand clasp and the words of welcome. Each wheel-chair occupant was personally greeted.

Now occurred one of the unscheduled events that showed the character of the Queen. Escorted by General Lord Frey-berg, she walked to the stand in which were seated the widows of the V.C. holders. Her informal short speech made this rather sad band of women part of the ceremony.

All the celebrities were there, but only to pay tribute to these men. Seated just below me was Sir Winston Churchill, looking his best and happiest. I walked down to him and said, "May I take your picture sir?" It was so unorthodox that one of the stewards rushed up to put me in my place. Said Sir Winston, "Don't bother the lady. She's a Canadian. Now just step aside till she takes my picture."

The royal wedding was romantic. The coronation was breath-taking. Runnymede left me with a feeling of proud sorrow. But the Victoria Cross Centenary re-established the fact that men of high courage still live in our world.

Following royal events at which I have been present, one of the questions most frequently asked is, "What is the Queen like as a person?" Let's face it. A ruling sovereign such as the young Queen, can never be a person. Both in public and private she is a symbol of state. This requires a high degree of self-discipline, to which Queen Elizabeth has been trained.

There has been criticism of the Queen's advisors, her public addresses and her manner of speaking. Critics claim that her advisors form a palace guard, that her speeches are stilted and that her voice sounds immature. Has anyone stopped to think that protocol is the backbone of international relations, that an "ad lib" interjection that might be highly popular in Washington would find a different interpretation in Ghana, the new member of the British Commonwealth? Or have we stopped to consider that the personal friendships of every member of the royal family may be misinterpreted? One of Britain's prime ministers, Lloyd George, neatly summed up the situation when he said, "The top of the mountain is lonely."

Those of us who have seen the young Queen under every circumstance know that with her a sense of duty, the dignity of the Crown is her paramount consideration. It was her destiny to become a queen, with a queen's tightly circumscribed life.

This thirty-one-year-old wife and mother can never go casually shopping as would you or I. She loves dancing, but she can dance only with carefully selected partners. She enjoys entertaining, but again guests must be so selected that no preference is indicated. She has inherited royal residences whose furnishings must not be changed. Perhaps the happiest period in the Queen's life was when, as Princess, she selected Clarence House as her official residence. It was she herself and Prince Philip who selected and arranged the furnishings. After the death of her royal father this halcyon period ended. Now it is Buckingham Palace with its historic traditions. She has no privacy either at home or in public. The policy of the British Commonwealth is carefully projected by her Cabinet; from that policy she must not deviate.

In her public appearances the Queen not only does the prescribed correct thing, but adds thoughtfulness. Notable are the gentle tone of her voice when she speaks to children, and her instinctive deference to the aged. It is here that the innate kindliness of the Queen's character shines through all formal procedure.

Chapter fourteen

In radio, anything can happen

E VERY broadcast is an adventure, the only difference being
that some are more hazardous than others.

We landed in Yorkton, Saskatchewan, on the night
of its hockey duel with the neighbouring town of Melville. The
final and deciding game of a hard-fought series was being played
in Yorkton. Feeling ran high; Melville supporters occupied one
side of the arena while Yorkton fans were on the opposite side.
Melville won the game, the series and the trophy.

When the committee asked me to present the cup, I took it as
a courtesy and innocently walked out on the ice, trophy in
hand. Attempting to make a graceful presentation to the Melville victors, I was booed off the ice by the Yorkton fans. The
hard lesson learned: never get involved in hockey feuds.

Wind, weather and a tight schedule—you can't win every
time. This we discovered in our visits to the forty-four network
stations spread across Canada. Our time-table was set up to do
a well-publicized broadcast from each radio station. Only twice
were we not able to report, "Mission complete, operation successful." Instead these two broadcasts were done from the nearest
airport.

En route to Edmonton and delayed by head winds, I realized
we could never make the Oil City in time for the broadcast.
Winnipeg was our stop-over point. "All right," I said, "we'll
tape the morning broadcast at Winnipeg."

The radio engineer on the plane alerted the local radio-
station staff who in turn brought out to the airport both remote
equipment and operators. As we sped off the plane, the worried

captain warned me, "Twenty-minute stop-over, Mrs. A. Can you make it?" We had to.

At 2 A.M. the airport manager manfully tackled the commercials, while sound effects were provided by the roar of planes taking off from the airstrip. The warning signal was the voice of the loud-speaker, "Flight 227 now taking off for Edmonton from Gate No. 5. No smoking please." This announcement signed off the broadcast. Were our listeners bewildered? Not nearly so much as the station manager.

En route to Newfoundland we ran into the same weather conditions and the same problem. It was solved in the same manner. Pausing briefly at Sydney airport, with mikes and equipment set up on a couple of army cots, we did our broadcast. Guests, hastily recruited from fellow passengers, included a Western Union Telegraph supervisor, a Netherlands bride, a British actor, and a woman mink rancher. They were all good.

A piano for a remote northern Sunday-school! This was the request from a young eleven-year-old following a broadcast. During the depression a grandmother, whose son was on relief, wrote: "Dear Mrs. A: We have no money for Christmas presents. My small granddaughter has been sending letters to Santa Claus asking for a doll. Could some of your listeners help us?"

This letter we read on the air and received not only dolls but doll clothes and carriages, all of which were distributed. The thank-you broadcast was heard by a little eleven-year-old, home sick from school. She too took her pencil in hand, writing: "Isn't it wonderful the little girl got her doll! I'm too old to play with dolls but I do need a piano."

Tactfully I wrote the little miss saying, "I don't know how we'd get a piano to your home." Promptly another letter arrived. "Every week my daddy drives his truck into Toronto. It would be no trouble at all to pick up the piano. We're starting a Sunday-school at our farm house. It sure would be nice to have a piano." One day at a service-club luncheon I mentioned this incident to my neighbour. He laughed, looked thoughtful, then said, "Say, we've got a piano we're not using. Where does the little girl live?"

The piano was tuned, packed, and loaded into Dad's truck.

Along with it went a book of instructions, "How to Play a Piano in Ten Easy Lessons."

The grand opening of the Sunday-school coincided with the twenty-fourth of May holiday. Wrote the little girl: "It was wonderful. Everybody was here. I played "Jesus Loves Me" with two hands and "Onward Christian Soldiers" with one hand. The bass notes are hard to read."

I saw the Niagara Bridge tumble down like a pack of cards. One winter the ice jam in the Niagara River threatened the bridge. For days newspaper reporters and photographers hung over the parapet along the river, waiting for the crash. For them, as day followed day, it got a little boring: attention slackened.

Looking for a local-colour story for the broadcast, we drove over one sunny afternoon to Niagara Falls. When we arrived at the scene there was nothing doing, the bridge was still standing; the crowds were gone; reporters and photographers were snugly entrenched in a nearby restaurant. "Let's join them for a cup of tea," I said to my companion. "That bridge is going to last forever."

It was at this moment that the ice-encrusted bridge cracked like a pistol shot, then slowly collapsed into the river. Photographers and reporters flew out of the restaurant, but it was all over. Amazingly, the only picture recording that final collapse was taken by an amateur photographer who happened to be passing.

That was the luckiest cup of tea never poured!

Hurricane Hazel, which devastated both Canada and the United States, did a really thorough job at the Holland Marsh, thirty-six miles from Toronto. For years this fertile valley, with its rich black earth, had been drained and cultivated by European market gardeners from The Netherlands, Belgium, Italy, Poland and Germany. Their small houses had been built on the perimeter of the marsh and had been completely safe.

Then came the hurricane, the beating rain and the rising flood. Within a matter of hours every family was evacuated from the marsh to the neighbouring town of Bradford. Community feeding centres were set up and trailer camps established in which families lived while the work of salvage went on.

Our radio audience gladly sent blankets, clothing and food. Turkeys for the Christmas dinner and toys for the children were also provided by our listeners. In order to bring both givers and recipients closer together, we arranged a remote broadcast in the trailer camp at Holland Marsh. Our function was to provide the facilities for the broadcast; the Holland Marsh people provided the Christmas carols sung by the various national groups.

Because no building was large enough, the broadcast was done out of doors. The night was cold, with sleety rain falling. The microphones had to be sheathed with pliofilm. But sweet and clear were the familiar carols sung in Dutch, in Italian, in Polish. Last of all came the German children:

> Now thank we all our God
> With heart and hands and voices,
> Who wondrous things has done,
> In Whom His world rejoices.

I found it difficult to sign off the broadcast without a break in my voice.

Driving home, our broadcast trio was strangely subdued. After a long silence our announcer said, "You know, there are two kinds of courage, the courage in battle and the courage to face the long, hard pull. It's the second kind that we've seen tonight."

Do poultry farmers eat eggs? On another broadcast we got the answer to that question. Honouring Livestock Day at the Exhibition, we took on as our guest the wife of a poultry farmer. Free and easy, completely sure of her ground, she did a marvellous show. When she finished, amidst great applause, one of the manufacturers presented her with a handy little gadget, an electric egg cooker. She thanked him, turned it around in her hands, then turning to the audience said, "Is there anyone here who would like this egg cooker? In our house we never eat eggs."

Annually two Christmas broadcasts were done—the Good

Neighbours Club for single unemployed men, and the Harbour Light, one of the downtown ports of mercy maintained by the Salvation Army.

The Good Neighbours Club was located in an old double house in what had been a good residential district. At one time it must have been a charming, gracious residence. The marble fireplaces were still there, so too were the high-ceilinged rooms and the curved staircase.

Open daily, the club now served as a meeting-place for out-of-work older men, who were permitted to sleep in the hostels but were not allowed to remain throughout the day. Each Christmas our radio audience and our sponsor provided warm woollen socks, cigarettes, fruit, candy and food.

I found it disturbing to talk to these old craftsmen, unable to fit themselves into the modern tempo. With great pride each would produce worn, tattered documents which testified to his ability as a skilled workman. Many of them spent hours in the tool department of the large department stores, gazing at tools they no longer had the privilege of using.

We tried to make the party gay with Christmas trees, coloured lights, good food and entertainment. But over all hung that indescribable air of hopelessness.

This was a Christmas party, but tomorrow was coming. Into overcoat pockets would go the fruit, the sandwiches, the cigarettes, saved for tomorrow when again the world would have forgotten them.

The Harbour Light in downtown Toronto always had the open door, but particularly on Christmas night. No card of membership was needed, no proof of identity. The attitude of the Salvation Army was, "If you're tired and home-sick, if you're friendless and discouraged, spend Christmas Night with us."

It was our privilege to provide the food. It was the privilege of the Salvation Army to provide the more essential hope for the future, a fresh start, a new incentive.

Commissioner Wycliffe Booth had a touch on the piano that a famous band leader might have envied. When he started into the Christmas Carols the voices of the men were wavering and uncertain. Many there must have remembered happier days when these same carols had been sung with a family group. But as one carol followed another the voices strengthened, the stooped shoulders straightened, the eyes brightened. In that one brief hour hope was rekindled.

Chapter fifteen

Now it's one world

AN INTERVIEW with Mussolini . . . Christmas Eve in Bethlehem . . . the Hungarian border at midnight . . . Easter week in Washington . . . Korea's front lines . . . San Francisco's World's Fair . . . Flight from Shanghai . . . Clambake in Trinidad . . . Hitler's speech from the Chancellery . . . Holy Year in Rome . . . the Pan-Asiatic Conference . . . Pink elephants in Kenya . . . Roosevelt in Washington . . . Clement Atlee at Constitution Hall . . . such material is the life-blood of broadcasts.

The appetite of listeners for details concerning world events is insatiable. Since distance has now become negligible, it is possible to offer eyewitness accounts for their enjoyment. It was both the pressure of the broadcasts and my own questing mind that took me into world travel.

Through the years I have travelled approximately two million miles, and visited most of the countries of the world to bring back personal impressions of what makes the world tick.

Since I was on a flat-fee basis, my sponsors never questioned where or how I should travel; their attitude was, "So long as the listening audience remains at top level, it's Kate's business." Quite frankly, I spent too much of my fee on travel, but it has given me a knowledge of world conditions that has meant more to me than money in the bank.

During the summer broadcast recess of 1938 I went newsgathering in Europe. Now it appeared as if the Spanish Civil War were to be the opening phase of World War II. I went by ship on the old S.S. *Mauretania*.

Shipboard companionship is surprisingly intimate. By the first day out you know the names of the people seated at your table; during the second day you learn their business associations; by the third day you know every member of their families. But at our table were two young men, silent and withdrawn, who gave no information. They never mingled with the rest of us but kept themselves apart. On the passenger list they appeared as Mr. Smith and Mr. Brown of New York, which I was sure were only assumed names.

Travelling on a budget, I was located on D deck, deep in the bowels of the ship. One hot sultry night when the ship was pitching and tossing, I went on deck to get fresh air. Preceding me was Mr. Smith, obviously sea-sick. As he rushed to the rail a dip of the ship almost tossed him overboard. I caught him by the arm, steadied him, and tucked him into a deck chair. He claimed I rescued him from a watery grave, and warmed by this experience his icy reserve melted. An ebullient type at heart, he took me into his confidence.

At this time Spain, in the throes of civil war, had banned all newsmen and photographers. This pair of American adventurers had decided they could make an illegal entry into Spain, bootleg pictures, get them back to New York, and make money. "Take me along with you," I said. "This is real broadcasting material."

Mr. Brown, when approached, turned thumbs down on the whole proposition. "No ma'am," he said decisively, "dames talk!" His decision was made. It was useless to tell him it was only by talking I made a living.

But just before we landed at Southhampton, Smith and Brown totted up their expenses and decided that a little extra cash was necessary. Their proposal was that if I would contribute $300, they would take me along on this hare-brained expedition. I hadn't that much extra money, but I didn't hesitate a moment. Immediately we landed I cabled my brother, "$300 urgently needed. Please cable at once to Canada House."

Within twenty-four hours the money arrived, and with my cash in hand Messrs. Brown and Smith completed negotiations.

The flight over Spain was to originate from Paris on July 14th,

Bastille Day. Their instructions to me seemed straight out of a secret-service thriller. I was directed to leave the city at 5 A.M., and drive to Le Bourget airfield, then take another taxi and continue for three miles along the country road marked on the map. "At this point," said Mr. Smith, "you'll reach a farm with a barn standing right at the roadside."

Everything worked out according to directions. Hidden inside the barn was a small plane, a pilot, and my two companions. By seven o'clock we were airborne, with a pilot whose face I never saw. My two companions were equipped with movie cameras and binoculars.

We flew over the Basque coast, where pictures were taken of the fleeing refugees. We flew over Madrid during the first major air battle of this war. We arrived back in Paris in time for the Bastille Day celebrations; then picked up the late editions of the newspapers with black headlines, "TODAY 100 PLANES OVER MADRID."

Coming back by way of New York and while waiting for a flight home, I dropped into a movie theatre to see the news film. There, to my surprise, were the pictures of that Spanish adventure. Aided by my $300, Smith and Brown had pulled it off.

To see a tiny five-year-old who had escaped the unbearable horrors of war by retreating into a Never Never Land . . . to see him again become a normal child is a miracle. This I saw.

During World War II our radio audience supplied clothing for bombed war orphans in thirteen British nurseries. Visiting Great Britain directly after one of the shipments had arrived, I went to the nursery school directed by Miss Anna Freud, daughter of the famous psychiatrist. All the forty children in this old house just outside London were shock victims. Standing in the window of the big playroom facing the street was a blonde little fellow who kept saying over and over, "My daddy will soon be here. My daddy will soon be here." It was as if a needle were caught on a record.

"Who is this little fellow?" I asked Miss Freud.

She shook her head sadly. "His parents were killed in the raid on Manchester. Teddy was entombed for a whole day in the wreckage of their home. He is a lovable child, quite amenable, but can't quite grasp the fact that his parents are gone. He keeps watching for his father."

"Let's put one of the little dressing-gowns on him," I said to Miss Freud. Made of men's discarded woollen socks, they were as gay as Joseph's coat of many colours. When Miss Freud returned with the little dressing-gown, the boy stood submissively while the small garment was fitted on him. Then suddenly he came to life. Lifting the dressing-gown, he pointed to one individual pattern. "My daddy had a pair of socks like that," he said.

That tiny bit of colour brought back to the far-away eyes the light of reason. On such a frail thread do miracles hang.

The *Major Bowes' Amateur Hour,* when I started in radio, was to listeners Ed Sullivan, Bob Hope and Steve Allen all wrapped in one. Regularly at 8 P.M. Sunday night radios were tuned in to hear the Major extol the screech of violins made from tomato cans, elocutionists doing "Paul Revere's Ride," or a local band whose members knew they were as good as Guy Lombardo.

Searching for an interesting Easter broadcast, I planned a week-end which included the latest Broadway show, the Easter parade in Atlantic City, the Major Bowes radio show. On request the guest ticket for the broadcast was forthcoming, but to my surprise I was also invited to the supper party that followed. What to wear? Since Americans generally expected Canadian guests to arrive in Hudson Bay coats and snowshoes, I bought me an elegant formal dinner gown of green and gold brocade, with long sleeves and high neckline. Back-fastened, it had eighteen buttons from the neck to below the waist.

Sunday night I arrived from Atlantic City with just half an hour to change and make the broadcast studio. The suit was shed, the dress slipped on, but I was able to manage only three buttons at the neck and three at the waist.

I made the studio on time but the woman sitting behind me was much concerned with my lack of coverage. While the home-made violins see-sawed up and down with "Swanee River," she leaned over my shoulder to say, "Don't you find it drafty, dear? Would you like me to fasten your buttons?"

"Thank you," I said and was buttoned up.

Much warmer and feeling respectable, I thoroughly enjoyed both the show and the remainder of the eveting. Indeed, as the supper party progressed I became not only warm but hot. Said one of the guests, "So you're from Canada. My cousin, Billy Thomas, lives in Edmonton. Have you ever met him?" It was useless to explain that Edmonton and Toronto, my broadcast headquarters, were almost 2,000 miles apart. He added, "Now if you ever see Bill give him my regards."

Second most popular question was, "Is there much snow in Canada?" To most Americans Canada was still the frozen north —the outpost of civilization, where we lived in igloos, were knee-deep in snow the year round, and mushed to the American border by dog sled.

Berlin in July 1945 smelled of death. The heavy bombings of that year had destroyed 69 per cent of the city. Coffins were scarce and adequate burial grounds even scarcer. On almost every lawn humps of earth testified that there bodies had been hastily buried.

Although I was wearing the uniform of a Canadian war correspondent, I had been retained by the British Ministry of Food to do a survey of food conditions in newly liberated or conquered countries. This survey took me to Berlin.

During the first two weeks in July German refugees, expelled from the land they had expropriated in Poland early in the war, were coming home. It was the British who set up bread lines for this endless procession. My O.C. suggested that in order to get a complete picture I should do a three-day stint serving the rations provided—a bowl of soup, a slice of bread, and a wedge of cheese.

It was a memorable experience, which left me more perplexed than ever as to the complex character of the German people. This proud, defeated nation was still sentimental and arrogant, still self-centred and self-pitying. In those three days I heard no condemnation of Hitler, but much bitter resentment towards the enemy and the conviction that again, Germans had been put upon by an unkind world. The Hitler myth still continued, and indeed in the hearts of many Germans it lives to this day.

Going back to Berlin again in 1947, I found that the mass of rubble had been tidied up but building had not recommenced. The occupying armies of Russia, the United States, Britain, and France were the dominating features in the life of the populace. Food and clothing were scarce and industry at a standstill. But little bakeries, small restaurants, and open markets were clean, tidy and self-supporting. The natural thrift of the Germans had begun to reassert itself. Under the submissive exterior was the iron determination to re-establish Germany as a great nation. One need only look at the present prosperity of West Germany to realize that here is a people that can never be wholly conquered.

Leaving on the 1947 trip to Germany, I was loaded down with letters, photographs and gifts from the wives and sweethearts of the Canadian troops. "Try and see my husband," or "bring me back news of my boy friend," were the two most frequent requests. Then came the inevitable question, "Are German girls really attractive?"

On my return came one of the worst *faux pas* I've ever uttered. I assured our audience that husbands and sweethearts thought longingly of home, but added, "However there's no doubt that German girls are bending over backwards to please Canadian soldiers."

The response to this ad-lib remark was mixed!

To see the return of a son for years mourned as lost was another touching experience of the summer of 1945.

In July of that year one of the countries to which I flew was Norway. Reporting to the British airfield early one morning, I found myself in a line-up with thirteen Norwegian airmen, homeward bound after years of service in foreign lands.

When the lad behind me tapped me on the shoulder and said, "Hello Mrs. A., how's Canada?" my first question was, "Now where have we met, and what is your name?"

"Christmas, 1942, at Little Norway. I'm Nels. Don't you remember the party you had for us?"

It all came back—the Air Force barracks, the Christmas tree, and the young, home-sick Norwegians whom we entertained.

When Germany occupied Norway in 1940 not only was the Norwegian government-in-exile set up in London, but thousands of young Norwegians escaped to Britain, there to join the Norwegian forces reorganized abroad. For these young patriots Canada set up an air training base called Little Norway, which we frequently visited. Nels was one of our Canadian trainees.

On the flight to Oslo he told me his history. Escaping by night in a fishing smack, he and his four companions finally made Britain. From there he was transferred to Canada and had flown throughout the war. During these long years he had no word of home, indeed knew nothing of his family. Apprehensive of what lay ahead of him, he asked, "Will you come along with me until I see what happened?"

At the airport a jeep was provided for Nels, whose home was about forty-five miles from Oslo. As we drove there was little conversation. Occasionally he would say, "I wonder if my mother is still there?"

When we reached the lane leading to the farm-house, Nels could stand it no longer. Jumping from the jeep, he ran up the driveway as if on wings. The door of the white farm-house opened and his mother came out. Wordlessly they embraced one another. Said the driver, turning around: "Mission complete. Little Norway is home."

As we drove back to Oslo both the driver and I were quiet, seeing in our mind's eye that reunion. "For this my son was dead and is alive again; he was lost, and is found."

The uneasy peace that followed World War II was perhaps more upsetting than the war itself, since from it emerged no victors. Always a family given to incessant discussion, we thrashed over world events. My husband read deeply and constantly. Anne and Mary, both in University, were exposed to conflicting opinions. Because of the daily broadcasts, I followed closely every yellow news flimsy spewing forth from the teletype machines. One night while we were knee-deep in discussion, Anne said, "Do you realize, Mother, that my age group has never known anything but war and the rumours of war? Where will people turn for peace?"

"There's one spot," I answered, "where almost 2,000 years ago the ideal of peace on earth was proclaimed with the birth of Christ. I'm going to Bethlehem for Christmas Eve."

As usual, the decision was made before the difficulties to be surmounted were assessed. Israelis and Arabs were virtually at war. It was easy enough to get air passage to the young state of Israel, but how does one cross into the Arab state of Jordan? Even Jerusalem was cut in half, part belonging to the Jews and part to the Arabs.

On Christmas Eve, movement for pilgrims across the border was permitted, but only between certain hours and with a special visa. My journey through the Mendelbaum Gate meant producing visas on the Israeli side, then an uneasy walk across no man's land with its barbed-wire entanglements and road blocks. Again came the rigid inspection of visas, this time by Arab officials. Then followed the long drive to Bethlehem. In the darkness lights twinkled in the valleys below. But the pale moonlight also shone on the guns of troops stationed on both sides of the border. "Peace," I thought, "can it be found here?"

The little town of Bethlehem was bitterly disappointing. Its two main streets looked like a midway. Shops filled with curios were blazing with light and importunate sellers of mother-of-pearl crosses besieged every pilgrim. But when we crossed the square to the church, when we stooped to enter the narrow door, the pageantry of 2,000 years was "like a bright and shining sword in the hand of the Lord."

The scarlet, purple and gold vestments of the priests, as they went in procession to the altar, the bemedalled uniforms of the representatives of the United Nations, blazed with colour. But far more significant was the intense quiet of the 2,000 worshippers. Standing packed together, their faces a white blur in the candlelight, they scarcely seemed to breathe. Here in Bethlehem on Christmas Eve, hope was reborn.

Cooking bacon and eggs in an unpressurized transport plane at 10,000 feet was one incident on my trip to Korea. Canadian servicemen stationed in Korea were not too happy, and so informed their relatives at home. Canada's Minister of Defence decided that an eyewitness account might perhaps clear the situation and ease the minds of the home folks. I was permitted to fly the northern route from Tacoma to Tokyo with the famous Canadian Thunderbird Squadron. From Tokyo to Korea I was on an American plane. This regular air service flew mail, medical supplies, spare parts and replacements four times weekly.

Since I was the only woman flown on this transport service, I was listed as a member of the crew. The big DC-4, stripped down to the bare bones, was unheated, unpressurized, uncomfortable, but safe. We took our own food on board, consisting mostly of bread, bacon, eggs, tea and coffee.

Just before take-off the young captain in charge of the flight said, "This is a pretty busy flight, with no time off for anyone. Our custom is to assign one member of the crew to galley duty. We all drop our names in a hat and the first pulled out sees to it that bacon-and-egg sandwiches and a hot drink are both available on the whole flight." My own conviction is that every slip had my name on it. I couldn't miss.

The galley? It was a tiny little passage set between the cockpit and the baggage compartment. Indeed it was so narrow I had to go in sideways. The two-burner electric stove constantly held a huge pot of coffee and a pan of bacon and eggs. If you ever get bored with life or feel that it's passing you by, try making bacon-and-egg sandwiches with one hand while you hold an oxygen mask over your face with the other. It's the neatest trick of the week.

Monday morning in Korea was not too much different from Monday morning at home. Brigadier Rockingham saw that I got to the Canadian front lines, since, as he said, it was a quiet day. The men took advantage of the lull to do their washing and take a bath. Consequently, barbed-wire fences were strung with socks, shirts and underwear.

The complaint of these boys, so far from home, was that they didn't get nearly enough home mail, home newspapers or home magazines. Food was plentiful and good. But it didn't take the place of news of local happenings. Directly I returned we started a campaign, "Send your home-town newspaper to your home-town boy." Hungry for news, they read the social items and the advertisements.

How the Korean campaign will stand up in history, no one can yet determine. But to the average soldier it was a frustrating, abortive effort.

Chapter sixteen

Famous people make news

TO INTERVIEW politicians very much in the public eye, I travelled thousands of miles. Such celebrities included the late President Roosevelt; Britain's Foreign Secretary Ernest Bevin; the Governor of Cyprus, Sir John Harding; Australia's Prime Minister, Robert Menzies; Canada's all-powerful C. D. Howe; Lady Nancy Astor and Jenny Lee, whose backgrounds were so different; and Adlai Stevenson, presidential candidate. Were these people hard to interview? Not at all. Naturally they were guarded in their policy statements, but our audience could read all that in the newspapers. Listeners were more interested in the impact of each personality during an interview, the setting, the clothes worn, and the casual remarks.

The interview with President Roosevelt took place just after the formation of the Civilian Conservation Corps which, during the depression, gave employment to jobless young men. Arriving in Washington for a late-afternoon appointment with the President, I was told that A.F. of L. president William Green was with him. Since their discussion had been completed, I was invited to join the gentlemen in the President's office. Although their views were divergent on many points, they both agreed on the vital necessity of helping the youth of the country.

Ernest Bevin was one of the most colourful characters I have ever interviewed. In 1940 Churchill, his friendly enemy, persuaded him to become Minister of Labour in the war-time Cabinet. On Ernie's shoulders rested the heavy responsibility of the production of war material. Speaking the language of the workers, he was eminently successful.

When in July 1945 his own Labour Party swept into power in Great Britain, Ernest Bevin became Foreign Secretary. Post-war labour adjustments, complicated with international politics, were his hard task. Even then he was convinced that Russia was a force to reckon with.

His custom was to eat his lunch alone in the House of Commons restaurant, surrounded by maps and memos. When I asked for an interview he was not too cordial, but finally said, "Come along and have lunch with me. I can give you fifteen minutes." The lunch consisted of bread, cheese and beer. But the priceless comment which I carried away was his remark concerning Vishinsky on Russian aggression. "I gave it to 'im fair!" This was the understatement of the year. Everyone knew that in this post-war period Ernie Bevin was the only man who could make the suave, polished Vishinsky red with anger.

The summer of 1945 I spent in Europe and came back to London for the British election returns in July. This was the election that swept the Conservative government out of power and the Labour government in, a complete surprise not only to the world but to the nation itself. That Churchill, in the hour of victory, should be rejected by the people whom he had led in the dark hours amazed everyone.

By seven o'clock that election night, the trend towards Labour was so obvious I went to the Labour headquarters. By this time everyone knew that Clement Attlee would be summoned to Buckingham Palace and there asked to form the new government. While Labour members roared with delight as each new victory was announced, Mr. Attlee sat on the platform, calm, composed and imperturbable. As usual he was tapping his notebook with his little gold pencil, the only visible sign of excitement.

Outside the hall a little English car pulled up, driven by Mrs. Attlee. "Clem," shouted the man beside me in the doorway, "your wife's here to drive you to Buckingham Palace."

Mr. Attlee walked through the cheering crowds as unassuming in victory as he had been in previous defeat. He climbed into the front seat of the car beside his wife. The modest little equipage, carrying the future Prime Minister of Great Britain, took off for the palace.

Mrs. Attlee, who accompanied her husband everywhere, took it for granted she too would be present at this important interview. However, she was stopped at the entrance to the palace. Undisturbed, she remained quietly outside in the car while her husband, in the traditional ceremony, accepted the responsibility of forming Britain's new government.

In spite of this new position and the light of publicity beating upon them, the Attlees changed their mode of living not one iota. A highly intelligent family, the two parents and their three children still pursued their quiet way of life surrounded by books and old family friends.

Seeking an interview with Mr. Attlee after a late session of the House of Commons, I was delighted when he suggested that I go home with Mrs. Attlee and himself. When we went in the house, it was as if we had entered another world far from the political arena. Mr. Attlee hung up his coat, settled himself in front of the fire, slowly sipped the one glass of sherry he permitted himself at the end of the day, and sank into silence. Prodded by questions, he would give me short, well-considered answers. From the point of view of background it was tremendously interesting; as an interview it was a washout. But I came away with the feeling that here was a man of integrity to whom position, personal honours and power were only the tools with which he worked for a welfare state.

Amongst women politicians interviewed, Lady Nancy Astor and Jenny Lee presented the greatest contrasts. American-born Lady Astor represented the constituency of Plymouth-Sutton in the House of Commons from 1919 to 1945 . Since Lord Astor was Mayor of Plymouth from 1939 to 1944, she was also Lady Mayoress of that city.

Although her public utterances were laced with spice and vinegar, her remark which I most remember was this, "Any woman who goes into public life should always wear a navy suit with a white blouse. It marks her as a lady."

Jenny Lee, wife of the fiery Labourite Nye Bevan, was not

so much concerned with looking like a lady as with acting like a human dynamo. Coming from a mining constituency in Scotland, she consistently fought for the welfare of women and children.

During the height of the trouble in Cyprus I flew to that little island to see if an impartial observer could make head or tail of the uprising. This small island, a British Crown colony in the Mediterranean, lying closer to Turkey than to Greece, was a hotbed of insurrection. Greece demanded its return to her, since 70 per cent of the population was Greek and only 30 per cent Turkish. Turkey opposed this move, as did Britain. The British Foreign Office regarded Cyprus as an essential military base for the protection of her interests in the Middle East. Cypriot terrorists made of the island a nightmare of uncertainty.

Flying from Athens to Cyprus were only seven passengers, two of whom were a British staff doctor and his wife, returning from a holiday. We arrived close to midnight, but since I needed background material both the doctor and his wife were kind enough to be my guests for a late snack. Our table in the restaurant was close to an open window. In the middle of our discussion a terrorist bomb was tossed through the window and blew up a table beyond ours. Actually there was not too much confusion following the incident, but it left me a little shaken. Said the doctor, "That's Cyprus. You'll get used to it," and calmly finished his sandwich.

When I checked into the hotel the bellboy took me to a bedroom on the first floor. The windows onto the balcony were open. He pulled down the iron shutters, then as a matter of routine, checked the bathroom, the clothes closet and under the bed for home-made bombs. I slept lightly that night.

That was Saturday. Sunday morning I attended the early-morning service at the Anglican chapel. The Governor of the island, Sir John Harding, arrived in a bulletproof car. Before his entry into the church, the little edifice was thoroughly searched for bombs—the altar, the chancel, and every pew. Only after this careful inspection were the prayers for the day read. This rugged soldier had no comment to make on the various attempts on his life; that he took in the course of duty. As he said, he had "been sent to Cyprus to keep secure Her Majesty's domain."

The Honourable C. D. Howe, while Minister of Defence for Canada, was a man of strong action and few words. Any interviewer trying to draw him out was promptly squelched. It all added up to: "This is my opinion. Take it or leave it." We took it, and left no wiser than when we entered.

Robert Menzies, Prime Minister of Australia, had only one concern, the welfare of Australia. If the conversation tended to veer to world affairs, his invariable comment was, "Now let me tell you what that means to Australia." He was polite, never seemed hurried, never antagonistic; but we came away with the feeling that Australia and its future was the dominant passion of his life.

We also came away with bulletins. His desk was loaded with pamphlets on Australia, all of which he thrust upon us. "Read that," he'd say, "and then you'll begin to understand our position." The one thing to which he objected was the incessant playing of "Waltzing Matilda" every time Australia was mentioned.

An informal and unexpected cup of coffee with Presidential candidate Adlai Stevenson turned into a question-and-answer period. Meeting Mr. Stevenson early one morning in New York just before the 1956 election, I was asked to share a morning cup of coffee. "Wonderful," I thought, "now I'll get a real interview." It didn't turn out that way. Before I could get in one lead question I was deluged with enquiries about Canada, the industrial expansion, the mining boom, the future of Ungava, the new aluminum plant at Kitimat, the interest of Canadians in the American political scene. By the time Stevenson questions were answered, there was no time left for the Aitken questions.

From that interview I emerged with the recollection of having talked to a well-read, well-bred gentleman, from whom I had gleaned not one quotable quote.

General Eisenhower I had met in London and in Canada. President Eisenhower I met in Washington. Affable, pleasant, sincere, all these attributes belong to the President of the United States. But sitting in at a press conference at the White House is as frustrating as shadow-boxing carried to its ultimate. We must leave it to history to assess this General turned President.

An interview that perhaps left me with more profound misgivings than any other, occurred in Chicago. I had supper with a group of young university professors and, as always, we took the world apart—the rising power of Russia, the uneasy situation in China, the middle-of-the-road attitude of India, the declining financial power of Britain. After hours of discussion, I turned to one of the younger men and said, "What do you think is the future of humanity?"

The answer was the essence of pessimism. Said this forty-year-old, "I try not to think of it. So long as men remain as selfish and women as jealous as they now are, what hope is there?" Here was the considered opinion of a student of history and humanity.

Pink elephants! These I saw while on a Comet flight to South Africa. In Uganda we stopped off to visit a Canadian mine buried deep in that lovely country. The clearing around the main house had been hacked from the forest. Its tiny lawn was surrounded by a fence of sharpened stakes that made it look like a fortress of pioneer Canada. In this case, however, the palisade was protection against the wild animals that roamed the forest.

After supper my host said, "Would you like to go down to the river to see the elephants?" So down to the river we drove, left the jeep and climbed the trees. Perched there, we sat in absolute silence.

Presently the elephants came shuffling out from the tropical woods, so grey, so huge and so impressive that it seemed like a picture from *Grimm's Fairy Tales*. Wading into the water, they romped like children in a bathtub. Filling their trunks with water, they sloshed it over themselves, snorting and trumpeting in sheer ecstasy. When the fun was over they walked out on the river bank, whose clay was as red as the farms of Prince Edward Island. They rolled in it, tossing this way and that; and when they reared up on those huge legs, quite literally they were pink elephants.

Needless to say, no one descended the trees until the last shadow was swallowed up by the quick oncoming of the African darkness.

"Asia for the Asiatics!" This is not only a phrase, but a conviction, strong as life, fervent as religion. On one of my world tours I arrived in New Delhi, India, at the same time as the first full-dress Pan-Asiatic Conference. Seventeen nations of that vast continent were represented. There was one Anglo-Saxon, the delegate from New Zealand. As a travelling Canadian, I was permitted a remote seat in the balcony for one session.

To most of the countries there represented, self-government had been granted. Heady with success and intent on their destiny, speaker after speaker repeated the dominant theme, "The day of the white man in Asia is over." As one particularly fiery speaker envisaged the power of these nations, I stood up to get a closer look. Looking directly at me, the speaker repeated, "The day of the white man in Asia is over, so too is the day of the white woman."

Although this is hard to realize, it is so true. One phase of history has ended and another has begun. The work of foreign countries who moved into Asia, built railways and irrigated deserts, provided schools, universities and hospitals, is completed. Trade will continue, but on a different basis. Henceforth it will be equal talking to equal. The interchange of students, quick communications, world trade, and common problems have created a new world which is one world.

Holy Year in Rome, 1950, was another intensely interesting experience. That springtime the city was particularly beautiful;

the yellow mimosa bloomed so profusely and so early. The fragile blossoms hung like golden bells over every stone wall.

The personality dwarfing all others was that of Pope Pius XII, with whom I had an audience. The notification, complete with the Papal Seal, was delivered to my hotel only the night before the audience. At the appointed hour I was provided with an escort. We walked up the outside stairs of the Vatican, part of St. Peter's Cathedral; here we were admitted by the Swiss Guard. Another flight of stairs and we were passed by the Gendarme Guard. At the entrance to the first audience chamber, our credentials were again checked by the Palatine Guards. Here were the Vatican lackeys, in red velvet outfits with black buckled shoes. Finally we were ushered into the third audience chamber, beautifully hung in deep rose satin and with a rose rug. It was here we were received.

There were twenty-nine of us, from fifteen different countries. We had all been thoroughly briefed as to what we should wear, the men in business suits, the women conservatively dressed, with gloves off and no dangling handbags.

As we stood quietly, the Pope entered on noiseless, red-velvet-slippered feet. His white soutane, his small white ermine cape, his white skull-cap matched his pale, delicate face and fragile hands. Going quickly from one to another, he greeted each one of us in our own language.

When he came to me I had a personal request. One of the girls in our office was being married in June of that year. Her mother had given her a bridal rosary. Holding it in my hand, I told him the circumstance and asked that it be blessed for Lucy. After the blessing he added, with a gentle twinkle in the eye, "And may all her children be healthy and happy."

Beside me stood a family group, a mother and her two children from Chile. The eight-year-old boy was soberly attired in a black suit, white wool stockings and black shoes. But the six-year-old daughter of the house looked like a fairy. She was all in white, with a floating veil, long silk stockings, tiny kid shoes, and fingerless gloves. When she knelt for her blessing the Pope said very gently, "Are you a good girl, do you do your lessons, do you obey your parents?"

"Si, Holy Father," she answered, her dark eyes shining.

The mother's eyes filled with tears, "Here," she said, "is a blessed child."

Princess Margaret and the humming-birds, both of them gay and brilliant, were part of the scene in Trinidad, 1955. As usual with these royal tours, every occasion had been so carefully planned that no slip-up was possible.

Before the tour wives of officials shopped feverishly for suits, afternoon dresses and glamorous evening clothes. Following the pattern of the island, these outfits were charming but conservative. The suits were classically cut and impeccably tailored; afternoon dresses were conventional; no dinner gown was cut to the waist in the back, and the front exposure was moderate.

Of all the formal occasions, the most exciting was the ball at Government House. When the young princess, looking stunningly beautiful, appeared in a gown which seemed suspended in defiance of gravity, the gasp of surprise was quite audible. Indeed, so great was the impact that at home, surveying pictures of the occasion, members of the House of Lords discussed it quite solemnly. But from that momentous night, dresses in Trinidad dipped lower. Dressmakers, equipped with scissors, did a masterly job of renovation.

The event that seemed to impress Princess Margaret most deeply was the reception on the neighbouring island of Tobago. Guests were received under the huge tree fronting the governor's residence. In the distance were the blue waters of the bay. Standing on the lawn, in the shade of the tree, stood the Princess all in pink. She was greeted by hundreds of native children whose stiffly starched white dresses, white hair-bows and short socks contrasted so dramatically with the golden brown skin. They looked exactly like chocolate sundaes on parade.

That same afternoon a disabled veteran in a wheel-chair was presented to Her Royal Highness. He told her of having been in service with her naval grandfather, the late George V. Absorbed, she listened to his story, which he interrupted by saying, "My, but you look pretty." Officialdom was shocked, but Princess Margaret flashed him the radiant smile that transfigures her face. Perhaps never in her whole life had she received such a spontaneous compliment.

The humming-birds? My hotel room fronted on the Royal Botannical Gardens. Arriving early, I asked to have my breakfast served on the balcony adjoining my room. The large glass of orange juice on the tray attracted a pair of humming-birds from the gardens below. While I unpacked, the two brilliant little birds perched on the edge of the glass and sipped this nectar. When I walked to the doorway, with a whirr of tiny wings they were off. I felt that I had been welcomed to Trinidad.

The Golden Gate International Exposition at San Francisco, competing for a place in the sun with the New York World Fair in 1939, in my opinion won hands down for beauty, originality and pageantry. But in spite of Treasure Island, the parades, the lighting effects and the general *décor* of the city, it was the children who stole the show.

Four thousand youngsters, recruited from schools up and down the state, put on a massed festival of song. Trained separately and with only one rehearsal together, they gave a truly finished performance, all the more beautiful since it was held in the vast out-of-doors auditorium. The applause was ear-splitting and the attendance phenomenal.

But this journey to the West Coast included a more serious note. The previous year Mexico had seized and nationalized both American and British oil companies. This seizure, although strongly protested by both Britain and the United States, still remained the policy of the Mexican government. In this uneasy summer of 1939, rumours were afloat that German tankers were being refueled off the coast of Mexico with oil which both American and British oil men felt belonged to them. A scout plane, equipped to take aerial pictures, was sent out from San Francisco, and I was included on the flight. The evidence brought back could not be disputed. This unhappy liaison between Mexico and Germany had its own bitter aftermath. In 1942 German submarines sank Mexican ships, after which Mexico declared war on her one-time customer.

Rome, Madrid, London, Paris, Berlin—these and other places I have seen both before and after the devastation of war. But most poignant and heart-breaking was the Austrian-Hungarian border following the ill-fated October revolution of 1956.

A month after the initial uprising, I flew to Vienna to report on the actual conditions of the Hungarian refugees and the help needed. Arriving in the city at twelve noon, at 12:30 we started our survey of the refugee hostels situated within the city. Empty houses, unused buildings and an abandoned castle were all in use. Vienna, the home of beautiful women and Strauss waltzes, only lately released from Russian domination, had over-night become a city of mercy. At five o'clock each evening a voluntary exodus from the city took place. By devious routes, cars, station wagons and trucks moved from the city to take up their vigil on the border. Throughout the long night these volunteers picked up the escapees and rushed them either to the first-aid hospitals behind the line or to the transit camps scattered throughout the countryside.

My multi-lingual driver knew every back road leading to the border. When we arrived at our point of watch the car was blacked out and left in a getaway position. At the edge of the marsh that separates Austria and Hungary we stood waiting for the rustle in the grass which might mean an escaping refugee. No word was spoken, no cigararette was lit. The minutes seemed endless.

Then came the sound for which we had been waiting. Said Franz, "Someone is crawling through the marsh." In tense silence, we strained eyes and ears. After what seemed an etern-ity the figure of a man on hands and knees did emerge. We picked him up, desperate, wounded, almost unconscious from loss of blood. Crossing the border, this twenty-seven-year-old Hungarian had been shot in the knee but had managed to crawl to safety. We rushed him to the first-aid post where doctors and nurses waited for just such emergencies.

Later that night we picked up a little three-year-old whose mother had previously escaped to Vienna. Smuggled to the border by an elderly neighbour, the child had her mother's name and address, written on pieces of cotton sewn to her garments.

But most devastating of all were the two boys, eleven and fourteen, whose parents had manoeuvred their escape. You might wonder why any parent would willingly part with children. One method to crush the revolution was this: if parents in Hungary were suspected, sons between the ages of twelve and twenty, and daughters from fourteen to twenty-two, could be seized and deported to labour camps. Frantic parents felt that even the uncertainty of escape by the children was preferable to the risk of deportation.

When the boys came whimpering over the bank like animals, they were incoherent. Rushed to the first-aid station, they were given a sedative. When we called back to enquire about them, the doctor said, "Hiding under a bush just on the border, they were flushed by a guard. It was either kill or be killed. They choked him to death." Haunted by this story, I asked the doctor, "Will they ever forget this experience?"

He paused briefly, looked out the window. "I don't know," he said, "but what you North Americans must remember is that these children have grown up in a police state where there is no security for happiness or normal living."

Security . . . happiness . . . normal living. How must it feel to walk out of your home and close the door behind you, leaving forever the familiar sights and sounds, the table at which you ate, the clothes you had worn, the garden you had tended; leaving the radio turned up, so that neither police nor neighbours should suspect that you were striking off into darkness and an unknown future.

The story of the Hungarian revolution is well known. Returning from Vienna I felt that no sufficient credit had been given the small country of Austria, itself newly freed from Russia and impoverished. With no thought of the cost, refugee camps were set up and thousands of people were fed and provided with clothing. When the need arose, in Austria the fountain of mercy overflowed.

Chapter seventeen

More honest pennies

W HEN TV became a potent advertising medium, my sponsors asked me to take on both radio and TV. Since TV was much more expensive than radio, it was decided that one weekly show was all that was feasible. On this variety show my responsibility was to do the food commercials.

It was great fun but it had its problems. To the artists the commercial was just a pain in the neck; to the sponsor it was the pot of gold that paid the bills. Many times I have seen the sponsor drowse quietly through the dance routine, only to come wide awake with the commercial. That he watched with an eagle eye.

Since in a half-hour show only so much commercial content may be included, it meant split-second timing. No easy ad libs here, but rather sticking strictly to the script, which had to be timed over and over again. Booming from the control room would come the voice of the commercial producer: "Cut that pause," or "Take out line three," or "Speed it up." Sandwiched in between a Calypso band and a blues singer, our commercials had to punch right in.

But the spoken word had to be pictorially strengthened with a display of food, not only attractive but with a new slant. In that picture must be a basic, practical idea, dressed up so that it could be utilized either for a family meal or for entertaining. And cameras, we learned, did strange things, not only to people but to Swiss steak. To get the right camera angle, food was prepared for the rough dress, for the dress rehearsal, and for the actual show—a triple operation. When we came to the real thing, a roast chicken must be fresh from the oven so that the golden brown skin was unwrinkled. Toast? On the show it had to be hot from the pop-up with never a curled edge. Spinach, lettuce and parsley, so beautifully green in real leaf, were simply black gobs when caught by the TV cameras. Indeed TV food was as carefully scrutinized as were the ballet dresses of the dancers. For this ordeal under the hot lights foods had to be reinforced with gelatine; for whipped cream we substituted shaving cream. No well-browned steaks went on TV, since under the camera they looked like old leather. Instead meat was briefly seared so that it should look good enough to eat.

Backgrounds for the food commercial had to be attractive but not too cluttered. After all, we weren't selling that pot of ivy hanging on the wall, but the food itself. Because of the glare of the lights on shiny surfaces, silver serving dishes and utensils had to be sprayed. One night when we were doing holiday buffet refreshments, I brought my best Crown Derby to add an air of elegance. All it did was confuse the issue; on camera the bold pattern of the china swallowed up the food. After that we stuck to plain, strong-colored dishes, extras instead of leading ladies. We learned, too, that good damask linen picked up a glare, so food was placed on dull-surfaced cloths. The appointments had good lines but no distracting decoration.

Clothes, make-up, hairdos, also had to be fitted into this pattern. Black, red and white did not photograph well. A uniform looked too much like a hospital, a house dress too informal, and a cocktail dress too elegant. At last we settled for tailored suits, whose collars and cuffs had to be dyed pale blue in order to look white on camera. To finish the picture a string of pearls and pearl ear-rings were added. (Brilliant jewellery flares under the lights.)

Because of last-minute catastrophes many sponsors have gone to filmed commercials as well as filmed shows. They're safer but not nearly so interesting. There's something about the voice of the producer saying, "Ready; on the air in three minutes," which alerts every performer. When the show is done on film the sense of urgency which makes every performer give his best is lacking. A filmed production is a long-drawn-out, repetitious affair which frequently lacks spontaneity.

When people ask me, "Isn't TV exhausting?" my response is: "It's just show business." However there is this difference: On the stage we can move about freely, knowing that every action is visible and every word heard in the farthest part of the theatre. In TV we must work within a narrow frame; a hand raised too high looks as if it were chopped off at the wrist; the eyes, because of close-ups, must always be fixed straight ahead so that the performer looks as if she were talking directly to each viewer. A sideways twist of the head means that the sound boom hanging above doesn't pick up the voice. But with all its limitations, TV is an exciting medium reaching into the homes of thousands of people to whom theatres may be inaccessible.

Its perils? That faces, mannerisms, types of speech become so well known as to become monotonous. A stage show can travel from continent to continent, with a fresh audience each night. Any repetition on a TV show probably brings the remark, "I've seen that before. Wouldn't you think they'd get something new?"

Here in TV is the greediest medium of entertainment, gobbling up talent, ideas, personalities.

For business women, beauty is not a cult but a necessity. No employer, no sponsor, no client, no group of women whom they meet, wants to see them looking untidy, unpressed and unpowdered.

One of the best-groomed women I have known was authoress Mary Roberts Rinehart, who always looked as if she had stepped straight from a bandbox. One of the tenets of her life was that even the busiest woman has time for personal care. Her favourite illustration concerned a prominent woman who always appeared in public slightly dishevelled, thinking this a mark of intellectual superiority. Said Mrs. Rinehart, "It was as if she said, 'Clothes, I'm going downtown. If you want to come, hang on!'"

After years of trying to get appointments at beauty salons on Saturdays when many shops were closed, I decided to do something about it. Checking not only with business friends, but with club presidents, busy mothers, and career woman, I found each one of them had a similar problem. Why not, I thought, set up a week-end salon where the whole business from hair-do's to pedicures could be done in forty-eight hours. Such a week-end periodically would be relaxing and provide adequate beauty care.

Following the decision came months of research and property hunting. I not only visited the best of beauty establishments but actually worked in them so that the knowledge was first hand. Diet was important and two types of diet were necessary —one for the guests who wanted to take off a few unwanted pounds, another for those who wanted to add curves. These diets were thoroughly tested on my long-suffering family, who rejoiced in the fattening diets and groaned through those first slimming diets. Gradually we worked out a low-calorie diet that not only took off weight but left the individual good tempered, with no drawn look on the face and no pangs of hunger.

While all this was in progress we bought a wooded property, about twenty-two miles from the city but as remote and quiet as a northern camp. To add the last touch of gentle beauty, a placid stream flowed between the hills which marked our boundaries.

Building was quite an extensive project, since it involved single bedrooms, adequate dining quarters, a comfortable lounge, an adequate kitchen, staff quarters, and the usual beauty rooms. Equipment was carefully selected, and so too were staff members.

Since this was never conceived as a great money-making project but as a service, we decided to limit the number of guests to twelve. This meant that each one would receive the personal, intelligent care so necessary to get the best results.

Selecting a name was as difficult as choosing the name of a baby with a lot of relatives. We tossed aside "Beauty Farm", "Harmony Haven", "Woodland Retreat", "Rest Acres" and similar names, and finally settled on a European name that we thought would be all-encompassing, "The Spa". This thoroughly perplexed the workmen who, until the day of opening, persisted in pronouncing the "a" as in "flat". Quite frankly, they thought the whole idea crazy, but to humour me went along with the gag.

We opened in late September, the ideal time.

The guests, checking in at four o'clock Friday afternoon, eyed one another warily, as women always do when meeting strangers of their own sex. You could see them mentally tabulating one another's cars, mink coats and luggage. We knew the arrival of everyone at the same time would make rather a strained half-hour, so we worked out the following technique.

Each single bedroom had been named after one of the internationally known spas. On the outside of the doors were hand-painted plaques with such names as Reykjavik, Iceland; Bath, England; and Hot Springs. There was also a picture of each spa. Inside, the bedrooms were done in pastel shades—pink, yellow, soft green, ivory, orchid, and grey.

Our smart young hostess, checking in the guests, would say, "Ah, I think we'll give you Wiesbaden. It exactly suits your personality. Michael will show you to your room." Intent on seeing how her personality had been transformed into lathe, plaster, paint and hangings, the guest sped on her way.

In each bedroom closet were placed the white terry-cloth robe, the soft slippers, the cosmetic bag, and the exercise outfit used by the guests. Directly the unpacking was done and the robe and slippers donned, each guest reported to the doctor for a thorough medical check-up. The reaction was amazing. Women who for years had dreaded going to a doctor lest the ache here or the pain there was really serious, came out from that check-up smiling and relaxed.

Now they had something in common. Over a cup of tea in the lounge, one would say to another, "My dear, he says I'm as healthy as a horse. All I need to do is cut down on my starches." The underweight type would exclaim, "Fancy me drinking a quart of whole milk every day! But that's what the doctor advises." You could see the baker calling less frequently and the milkman with a steady order.

After the medical, the shampoos began, for our hair specialist maintained that hair could be more perfectly dressed if there was an interval of a few hours after the shampoo. Then came a deep massage, followed by complete cleansing of the face, neck, hands and arms.

As they waited for dinner a non-fattening cocktail was served. While sipping they learned one another's names, where they lived, the husbands' professions, how many children—all that sort of thing.

The Friday-night dinner was more like a college reunion than anything else. Since all were going back for further treatment after dinner, they ate in their white robes, hair tied up in bandanas. It was quite a contrast to see the formal, candlelit dinner-table surrounded by what seemed a group of happy, chattering girls in strictly informal clothing. Since they all looked alike there was no need to keep up any pretense; the barriers were down.

Before going to bed the hair was well brushed, the face cleansed and the finger-nails oiled. Ten o'clock was bedtime. From room to room the two Finnish masseuses would go to give the final back-rub. Saturday morning when the breakfast trays were served, the remark most commonly heard was, "I slept like a baby. Do you know, I haven't had a sleep like that for years."

The Saturday routine included exercise, a walk in the woods, massage, Scotch hose treatment, manicure, pedicure, facial, and the dressing of the hair. To the Saturday-night dinner husbands and sweethearts were invited. By the time they arrived these fresh-skinned, immaculate beauties were radiant in evening gowns. When the arriving husbands looked round this bevy of attractive women, each would exclaim, "Now which one of you is my wife?"

There was no difficulty with the dinner-table conversation—it sparkled and flowed. When our men guests left at 11 P.M., it took another hour of face-cleaning and back-rubbing to get everyone in the mood for sleep.

On Sunday, breakfast, again in bed, was an hour later. We had checked to find which church each guest wished to attend. It must be conceded that the guests from "The Spa" rated almost as much attention from the congregation as did the minister.

After Sunday dinner we had a class in make-up. Seated in front of individual mirrors with the cosmetics selected by our beauty expert, each woman put into practice the things she had learned. By now they were completely unselfconscious and applied the make-up with all the care and exactitude that an artist gives a masterpiece. Such remarks would be passed as, "I never knew before how to make my nose look smaller," or "That deepened line on my lower lip certainly looks good, doesn't it?"

The week-end concluded with high tea served at five o'clock, to which again the men and guests were invited. At these tea-parties there was always some new gimmick introduced. The guests would put on a fashion show, or demonstrate their exercises, or—most amusing of all—exchange hats and do a millinery exhibit.

When they said goodbye, not only had the guests themselves struck up lasting friendships but we had made new friends. To me it was most gratifying when guest after guest would say, "I feel ten years younger," or "You know when I came on Friday, I was right at the end of my tether. But now I feel as if I can face anything." To these busy women, this forty-eight hours was like an ocean voyage. They were babied, pampered and completely cut off from their normal heavy responsibilities. No meals to get, no dishes to wash, no phones to answer, no children to discipline, no decisions to make. The letting down of tension meant almost as much to them as the newly styled hair, or the flattering make-up.

Who were the guests? Business women, professional women, club presidents, private secretaries, brides-to-be and their mothers, librarians, and teachers. One thoughtful husband, in a family where there were four young children, sent his wife once a month to give her a break from her routine.

Was it an expensive project to set up? Indeed it was. The building had to be spacious and beautiful. In order to give the proper setting the grounds had to be landscaped and maintained. The equipment was costly. China, silver, crystal, linen and food all had to be of the best. A double supply of blankets, sheets, pillows, pillow-cases, and towels must be always kept on hand.

Was this establishment costly to maintain? A staff of twelve was necessary, one for each guest. Since every member of the staff was an expert, salaries were high. But it was one of the most rewarding and diverting enterprises on which we embarked. We all loved it. When the last car had driven away, we sat down and recapitulated the whole week-end. There was never any griping from the staff, nor did we at any time have an unpleasant client.

But there was one week-end that topped all others. At this time I was doing a great deal of work amongst old-age pensioners. In a moment of exuberance I suggested that we should set aside an early summer week-end for twelve senior citizens. The selection was left to the various welfare organizations.

We picked them up Friday afternoon—the youngest seventy-one, the oldest eighty-two. They got the full treatment, even to make-up.

But it was the Saturday-night dinner that entranced us. The boy friends were of similar ages, but gallant as young beaus. After dinner when we went to the lounge I said, "Now what would you like to do?" Said a white-haired, fragile little lady, "Let's turn on TV and look at the wrestling matches. They're always so exciting on Saturday night."

My father owned a general store in a small village where he had two strong competitors. The store he loved, and the customers were to him not only customers but friends. But the chore he hated worst of all was writing the weekly ad for the local newspaper. He would put it off and put it off until the printer, quite desperate, would say, "Just give me a few items, Robert, and I'll write the ad for you." But father found an "out". When I brought home my report card with a high mark in composition, he decided that thereafter I should write the ads. The high-level reason I was given was, "You know, Kate, it's good training for you." The real reason was that it took this dull task off his hands.

For me it was anything but dull. It took a day of prodding to get the items from father that he wanted stressed. Followed a night's hard work to get it written. Was my father ever satisfied? No! Reading over the copy, laboriously hand-written on ruled paper, he would say, "Not strong enough! Pringle's and Reynold's can do better than that. Now try it over again." Father's idea of a real snappy ad was one that hit the customers between the eyes and had plenty of adjectives. "Throw in the adjectives," he would say. "One isn't enough. And don't forget the capitals."

So, after trial and error, I learned to write ads such as this:

Don't Shop Just Anywhere!
GO TO ROBERT SCOTT'S FAMOUS EMPORIUM
for
New . . . Astonishing . . . Breath-taking . . . Price-cutting
BARGAINS
High Class Goods will be Slaughtered Without Mercy!!
Extra Special Prices Paid for Butter and Eggs

Father gave this effort full marks. He claimed that in advertising superlatives bring in trade, and that restrained copy should be reserved for slick publications.

The writing field widened. Always in our small village we had teachers leaving for better posts, ministers being transferred to different churches, or young couples embarking on matrimony. Each occasion meant a farewell party, a presentation and an address. The writing of these addresses fell to my lot. Here too a technique was gradually developed. To the departing teacher it was: "Although it is with great reluctance that we say good-bye to you, the memory of the precepts you have instilled in us will always remain as a steadying influence in this community. As a small remembrance of our happy relationship, will you please accept this inkpot."

For the transferred minister the words varied, but the same basic thought was there: "In any future charge we know that you will give the same inspiration to the young, the same gentle consideration to the sick, and comfort to the dying. Our loss will be Cookstown's gain."

The address to the bride and groom was on a lighter note: "To you young people embarking on the sea of matrimony, all good wishes for a smooth, happy voyage. May all your troubles be little ones."

I got to the point where I could write those speeches blind-fold. If at any time a different note was interjected it was always crossed out, with the explanation, "I like the old speech better. It seems more fitting."

By this time the fascination of words had gripped me. I read everything I could get my hands on—almanacs, school books, library books, the daily paper, the local weekly, Sunday-school papers, and G. A. Henty's stories of adventure. When at sixteen I left home to go to school, the library in the collegiate had a steady customer. Our English master was a little concerned with my choice of books. *Lorna Doone, Jane Eyre and Cranford* —of these he approved. But when I delved into *Madame Bovary* he summoned me to a conference. After putting me at my ease by enquiring about my family, he asked, "Kate, do you read all those books you take home?"

"Yes sir," I said in a small, scared voice.

"What's the object of all this reading?"

Hesitating, blushing and almost incoherent, I mumbled my objective, "I'd like to write a book sir."

With an amused glint in his eye he gave me advice I've never forgotten. "Everyone," he said, "not only wants to write a book but is quite sure it can be done. A youngster like you has plenty of ideas, but putting an idea on paper is a long and difficult process. It's a professional job that takes knowledge, understanding and a sense of values. Forget the book until you've learned to think and to express those thoughts."

Some of this advice I understood, some of it went right over my head. But undaunted, and all through my life, I've kept covering scraps of paper with ideas.

If you have the desire to put words on paper, don't let anyone discourage you. But by the same token, don't try to write about something you've never experienced or places that you've never visited. As Women's Editor of a weekly magazine, my work included food, fashions, human-interest stories, the care and rearing of children, interior decoration, new trends in home-making, and advice to the love-lorn. This assignment came after I had struggled through young love, marriage, children, meals, clothes, painting and wallpapering at home, and trimming my own hats.

The vocabulary for each type of story is different, so first learn the vernacular. That means constant research, intelligent listening, and a feeling for the background. Once you've accomplished this, the phrases, the expressions are as comfortable and well-fitting as an outfit you love and in which you feel completely at home.

What is the most difficult copy to write? Definitely the most time-consuming and the most exacting is food copy. What you write is being read by women who've been preparing meals, or who expect to prepare them, all their lives. If, having tried your recipe, a reader is unsuccessful, you've lost a friend who will never trust you again. Food is too expensive to throw away. But as well as careful directions, women like variations on the main theme. I've always maintained that women don't get bored with cooking, but rather with making the same dish over and over again. So, even in the plainest recipe, it's essential to toss in a new slant, a different spice, or a different method of serving.

Hung in our test kitchen are our own Ten Commandments for efficiency:

Never publish a recipe that hasn't been tested at least three times. This triplicate testing establishes beyond doubt the ingredients, the oven temperature, and the finished product.

Always use standard-size pans and utensils. To help the young bride, include a line like "Bake in a loaf pan 9" x 5" x 3"," or "Bake in a two-quart casserole dish," or "Pour batter into two nine-inch round cake tins." Again to help the bride, we follow a recipe with a short footnote that says, "This batter is thin," or "This batter is quite heavy." This directive relieves her mind and, it could be, saves putting a flop before the young bridegroom.

Don't get so carried away that recipes include such exotic items as button mushrooms, ground hazel nuts, or cardamom seeds. Not only are they expensive but often not available.

Specify the kind of flour used. There are three general kinds—pastry, all-purpose, and cake flour. They all react differently.

Sugar should be similarly designated—white sugar, brown sugar, icing sugar, or fruit sugar.

Follow the food trends. Ready mixes, frozen foods, and ready-cut meats have altered food preparation to a remarkable degree.

Be precise with recipes. Ingredients should be arranged in the order of mixing. For easier mixing each separate movement should be in a sentence by itself.

Always include number of servings, or yield of cookies, hot biscuits or muffins.

With the meat recipes include a chart that shows the name of every cut and where located.

In reading cook-book copy, don't stay with it too continuously or table spoons will be confused with teaspoons. Without doubt it is the hardest copy in the world to check.

Words for cook-book copy—this is where the vernacular comes in. A cake should be moist, tender, delectable, light as a feather. A salad is appetizing, intriguing, attractive or crisp. Pastry should be flaky, puffy, golden-brown or rich. Gravy should be velvet-smooth and brown. Strewed occasionally through the copy can be such words as embellish, festive, pungent and titillating—but not too often.

There is something tremendously gratifying in compiling a cook-book. A well-tested one takes at least a year. But if it is well tested you know that it will stay there in the kitchen, be used day after day, and become a family friend. The pages on which the favourite recipes are printed will be stuck together with dough—a sure sign of success.

Covering fashion shows for newspapers and magazines opened up a new world of adjectives and a new side of life. A scientist who, after years of research, succeeds in finding a way to conquer a disease is not nearly so exuberant as a dress manufacturer who proudly displays his latest line.

My father would have enjoyed meeting these dress designers; like himself, they spilled adjectives as a fountain spills water. Evening clothes were spectacular; sports clothes were clean-cut; lingerie was fragile as a pink cloud; the unusual, expensive dress was precious. Through this dense foliage of words I gradually learned to find my way.

Amazingly, every season produced its own pet phrases. One season it would be "it's the gentle tempo". Then would follow "the dress that flows with the figure," or "elegance is back again." One year we went through a dreadful period when "functional" spread like an epidemic. Not only were clothes functional, but hands, furniture, houses, and hairdo's. To the fashion shows crowded women in plain tailored suits, stiff hats, and flat-heeled shoes—all functional. Happily this phase didn't last long; the fashion trend swung back with the greatest abandon to "luminous brilliance, soft-spoken grace, and silken luxury."

Writing fashion copy is somewhat like a game of chess. A list of appropriate words and phrases is compiled, and you move them about as the play demands. But even this type of writing fulfils its function. It not only acts as a guide to the well-to-do shopper but takes other women far from the routine of daily work to the fairyland of beautiful women and gorgeous clothes. After the supper dishes are done and the children put to bed, a busy housewife, who until now hasn't had time to sit down all day, will read entranced about early spring fashions which are "slender as a wand" or "pencil-slim". Mentally shedding her everyday clothes, she sees herself walking gracefully into a drawing-room with every head turning as guests exclaim, "Who is that attractive woman?"

Nonsensical? Not any more than her husband's dreams of some day becoming boss and being driven to the office in a Cadillac.

Writing fashion copy inevitably took me into commenting at fashion shows—another exciting experience. A well-styled fashion show is a magnet for clothes-loving women. Some come to buy—more come to see. Watching the faces of the audience as the svelte models sweep up and down the runway, a commentator can feel the current of thought flowing from the woman sitting in an aisle seat four rows back. You can feel her thinking, "Now I could take that old black velvet and make it over to look just as smart as that Paris model." And the extraordinary part of it is, in many cases she can.

Fashion photography was another avenue. Every dress designer wants his model to have chic, slender lines. Equally well he knows that any photograph apparently adds ten pounds to the model. Consequently a smart fashion photographer carefully studies the angles, reduces the avoirdupois, and accentuates the slender curves.

But essentially dress designers are warm, artistic people. A misplaced pleat, an unflattering neckline, the wrong fabric, or a poor colour will cause so much mental anguish that they develop stomach ulcers. But let them create a style that really clicks and they're kings of their domain.

When I started writing a Beauty Column I recognized certain basic facts. All women want to be considered the pursued and not the pursuing. A woman is reluctant to face the bitter possibility that a sweetheart or husband has become indifferent to her charms. Accordingly she will buy costly cosmetics and expensive perfumes, dye her hair, go on a diet, paste on false eyelashes, and use a chin-strap.

It's no use poking fun at these feminine foibles. The object of our column was to cater to them. So we invited questions from our readers as to their own personal problems.

After the column had been in existence for three months, a readership survey turned up the astonishing fact that readership wasn't entirely feminine; men also wrote in concerning their problems.

Feminine readership was divided almost equally amongst teen-agers, career girls, young matrons, the over-forty's, and those who were pushing sixty. Before we knew it we were involved in voluminous personal correspondence, which included such questions as:

I'm taking my girl to the high school prom. She doesn't like pimples and I've got them. How does a fellow get rid of them?

My hair goes oily three days after a shampoo. What shall I do about it?

Since Junior arrived my figure's all shot. How do I recover lost ground?

Although I'm only forty-five, my hair is prematurely grey. Should I dye it?

Have you a diet for a business executive with a spare tire?

My white hair has gone yellow at the sides. Should I bleach it or endure it?

This unending series of questions drove us to compiling a series of bulletins, which gradually grew into a book, *Lovely You*. Printed timidly, we discovered its sales were far beyond our expectations. Indeed the principal of one collegiate institute reproached me—he claimed his male students were reading it in their study periods.

Now we learned a new vocabulary. Women love such words as fragrant, smooth, vivid and alluring. Except for the small minority, seductive, dangerous and passionate really upset them. Two statements they enjoyed were "Beauty is something intangible," and "Any woman can be lovely."

But sometimes these columns boomeranged. An excellent slimming exercise we advocated was this: "Lying flat on your back, hands clasped behind the neck and ankles crossed, bring yourself to a sitting position; repeat twelve times."

To simplify the procedure, we added, "For leverage, tuck the toes under the radiator." One woman who tried it ripped the radiator from the wall, flooding not only her apartment but the one beneath. The landlord threatened us with a lawsuit.

In another column, following directions for a relaxing face-pack, I added "Quiet is essential. Take the telephone off the hook." The telephone company was not amused and wrote a stern reprimand.

From letters we found out that husbands with beauty-loving wives sometimes begrudged the modest sum spent on cosmetics. To counter this situation, we did a survey on how little it costs to keep a wife well groomed. We headed the column "You Can Be Lovely for 39c a Week."

While that edition of the paper was still warm from the presses, cosmetic advertisers phoned my boss to enquire in angry tones, "How can we make a living on 39c a week?"

But this service, quite as much as our food columns, we felt filled a need in the lives of most women. Young John Keats, who left this world almost 140 years ago without ever writing a word of good-grooming copy, put his finger on it: "For ever wilt thou love and she be fair."

Readers and listeners expect an editor or a broadcaster to know the answers to all problems. We were flooded with such questions as: Should the bride's sister have a shower for the bride? Are godparents expected to present christening gifts to the godchild? Do I curtsy to the Archbishop or shake hands? Who pays for the bride's bouquet? When I go out with my boy friend should I go dutch? Should wives be invited to office parties? Following a death, to whom should the flowers be addressed?

After years of answering such questions as this it seemed to us that there was a place for a common-sense book on everyday etiquette as it affected the average family. Was such a book in existence? To answer that question we did some research. The standard etiquette books, we discovered, dealt with situations that seldom exist for ordinary individuals. How many people are presented to the Queen? How many couples are entertained in a home with a butler? How often is the young suburban couple invited to a consular reception?

So in compiling our etiquette book we took people of moderate means who dine out occasionally, attend a theatre party once in a blue moon, and entertain modestly at home.

The outstanding occasion in most homes is the marriage of the daughter of the house. Here is one time when every last detail must be correct, every rule of conventional conduct carefully followed. In writing the etiquette book we devoted forty pages to weddings, trying to answer every question from "Have the parents the right to question the financial status of the bride-groom?" to "In what order does the receiving line stand?"

Funerals are another important occasion when everything must be done properly and in order. At such a time, maintaining the proper formality helps to carry the members of the family through those difficult days. But what is the correct conduct?

Home entertainment didn't pose too great a problem, since the essentials are warm-hearted hospitality, good food, and interesting people. But formal entertainment outside the home was a different matter. Should the wife or the husband follow the usher in the theater? Does the headwaiter seat the women guests, or do the gentlemen in the party? At a formal dance, does the husband dance the first number with his wife or with their principal woman guest? At a dinner party, do husbands and wives sit together or as widely separated as possible? At a woman's luncheon, is the guest speaker presented with her corsage before or during the function?

The writing of the etiquette book was the result of phone calls and letters covering all those situations about which people are in doubt.

Mentally we went to dozens of weddings, hundreds of parties and teen-age functions. We christened the baby, buried grand-father, enjoyed wedding anniversaries, accompanied wives to husbands' conventions, and taught the children table manners. Menus were prepared for each and every occasion; to complete the service, recipes were also included. We wrote addresses of welcome, thank-you speeches, letters of congratulation, and applications for jobs. We suggested methods for handling the tricky problem of fourteen-year-olds "going steady".

When this book was complete we thought we had covered every phase of the etiquette of ordinary living. But we were wrong. After the publication of the book, letters continued to pour in, saying in effect:

"Your book has been read with great interest, but there's one point you've omitted. Should my next-door neighbour, to whom my husband has not spoken for twenty years, be invited to my daughter's wedding?"

"My husband and I are celebrating our twenty-fifth anniversary next month. Should written invitations be sent, or would a notice in the paper be sufficient? If we adopt this latter course we'll be eaten out of house and home."

"My husband always insists on asking his two maiden sisters to every party we have. Frankly, they're just a pain in the neck. How would you get around that situation?"

"If I'm invited to a wedding reception and not to the wedding, do I have to send a gift?"

"On page 56 you seemed to refer directly to our family difficulties. Is it fair to make us a laughing-stock in this whole community?"

After months of such letters we suspected that the more conventional books on lords, ladies and butlers were perhaps abstract enough not to draw such highly personal mail.

But one series of letters we cherished. A young Swedish girl, newly come to this country, became engaged to a mining engineer. Since she had no relatives in this country, she was in doubt as to how the wedding should be conducted. Wishing to pay all respect to her future husband's family, but also desirous of maintaining her own dignity, she wrote asking for help. Since a similar situation was occurring in many parts of the country we used her letter, omitting names, on the radio broadcast. The wife of the Swedish Consul sent us a pair of hand-embroidered pillow-cases to be forwarded to the bride. A cosmetic firm asked for the privilege of providing a travelling case. A group of young business women made a gift of wedding silver. The young bride happily acknowledged the wedding gifts, and also provided our office with a few happy moments. She said, "Your etiquette book and your help have seen me through my engagement and my wedding. I am taking it with me on my honeymoon." Could an author ask for anything more thrilling than that?